READING SCRIPTURE *in* WESLEYAN WAYS

READING SCRIPTURE in WESLEYAN WAYS

Edited by
Frederick David Carr
and Brady Alan Beard

Nashville

Reading Scripture in Wesleyan Ways

Copyright © 2025 Abingdon Press
All rights reserved.

No part of this work may be reproduced or transmitted in any form or by any means, electronic or mechanical, including photocopying and recording, or by any information storage or retrieval system, except as may be expressly permitted by the 1976 Copyright Act, the 1998 Digital Millennium Copyright Act, or in writing from the publisher. Requests for permission can be addressed to Rights and Permissions, The United Methodist Publishing House, 810 12th Avenue South, Nashville TN 37203 or emailed to permissions@abingdonpress.com.

ISBN: 978-1-7910-3575-4

Library of Congress Control Number: 2025933192

Scripture quotations unless otherwise noted are from the New Revised Standard Version, Updated Edition. Copyright © 2021 National Council of Churches of Christ in the United States of America. Used by permission. All rights reserved worldwide.

Scripture quotations noted CEB are taken from the Common English Bible, copyright 2011. Used by permission. All rights reserved.

Scripture quotations from The Authorized (King James) Version. Rights in the Authorized Version in the United Kingdom are vested in the Crown. Reproduced by permission of the Crown's patentee, Cambridge University Press.

MANUFACTURED IN THE UNITED STATES OF AMERICA

Contents

About the Contributors ix

Introduction xi
Frederick David Carr and Brady Alan Beard
    The Nature of the Journey   xi
    A Road Map   xv
    For Further Reading   xvii

1. "The Way of Full Salvation": An Introduction to Wesleyan
Biblical Interpretation 1
Robert W. Wall
    Bible Study in and for the Church   3
    Wesley's Interpretation of Scripture   7
    Wesley's Theological Perspectives on Scripture   10
    The Goals of Wesley's Biblical Interpretation   13
    Toward a Wesleyan Theological Interpretation of Scripture   14
        Via Salutis   16
    Conclusion   18

2. Wesleyan Biblical Interpretation in the Age of AIDS 23
Cheryl B. Anderson
    The Prosperity Gospel: Definitions and Advantages   25
        The Prosperity Gospel and Its Disadvantages in the Age of AIDS 26
        The Prosperity Gospel, The Bible, and John Wesley   30

    Methodist Re-Readings of the Bible in the Context of HIV
        and AIDS   37
    Conclusion   41

3. Wesley's Ecologically Informed Interpretation of Scripture, Science, and Society 47
Presian R. Burroughs

    Wesley's Ecological Interpretation of Scripture   49
        Wesley's Attention to Nonhuman Creation in Scripture   50
        Wesley's Attention to Relationships and Cause and Effect   51
        Wesley's Attention to God's Redemptive Future   52
    Wesley's Interpretation of Scripture and Our Context   53
    Wesley's Ecological Interpretation of Science   55
    Wesley's Ecological Interpretation of Society   58
    Conclusion: A Wesleyan, Ecological Interpretive Framework   63

4. Reading Samson with Wesleyan Eyes........................ 69
Stephen Riley

    The Book as a Whole: A Sad Story in Three Movements   70
        Movement 1: The Miraculous Birth Gone Awry   72
        Movement 2: Broken Relationships   73
        Movement 3: Destroying Our Enemy?   74
    Judges as Part of Israel's History   75
        The Book of Joshua   76
        The Books of Samuel and Kings   76
        The History of Israel as Repentance Literature   78
    Reading the Text with Wesleyan Eyes   79
        Example 1: The Birth Story and Trusting God   79
        Example 2: Rashness, Broken Relationships, and Unrepentance   80
        Example 3: Destroying Our Enemies?   81
    Conclusion   82

5. God of Mercy, God of Wrath: Reading the Hard Parts of Scripture with the Early Church 85
Charles Rivera

    Drawing on the Riches of the Past: Four Views   88
        The Biblicist View   88
        The Modernist View   89
        The Traditionalist View   89
        The Wesleyan Christian View   89
    Understanding God's Mercy and Wrath with the Early Church   92
        The Heretics   92
        Origen of Alexandria   94
        Ephrem the Syrian   98
    Conclusion   101

6. 'A Conviction of Insufficiency': John Wesley's Approach to Old Testament Scholarship 105
Diana Abernethy

    "Searching the Scriptures" as a Means of Grace   106
    Fruits of Biblical Scholarship   109
    Fruits of Accessible Resources   112
    Fruits of Discipleship   114
    Reading Scripture with Wesley: Numbers 21:4-9 as a Case Study   116
    Conclusion   120

7. Drawn from the Waters: A Wesleyan Interpretation of New Birth in Exodus 2:1-10 in Conversation with Philosophical Hermeneutics 125
Kristin Helms

    Wesley, Philosophy, and the "Plain Meaning of Scripture"   126
    Exodus 2:1-10 and New Birth   127
    A Very Brief Sketch of Philosophical Trajectories Since Descartes   128
    Cognitive Metaphor Theory (CMT)   132

The Birth of Moses Meets Conceptual Metaphor Theory　　134
　　　Conclusion　　142

8. On Dogs and Difficult Texts. 145
Jennifer S. Wyant
　　　Wesley's Method　　146
　　　Paying Attention to the Text　　147
　　　Listening to Those Experienced in the Things of God　　154
　　　Conclusion: What I Learn . . . I Teach?　　159

About the Contributors

Frederick David Carr, Ph.D. is an Associate Professor of Biblical Studies at Northeastern Seminary at Roberts Wesleyan University and an Instructor for the Deaconess and Home Missionary program in the United Methodist Church.

Brady Alan Beard, Ph.D. is Head of Research and Instruction at Pitts Theology Library and an adjunct instructor at Candler School of Theology at Emory University, and he teaches for their Course of Study program.

Robert W. Wall, Th.D. is the Paul T. Walls Professor Emeritus of Scripture and Wesleyan Studies at Seattle Pacific University

Cheryl B. Anderson, J.D., Ph.D. is a Professor Emerita of Old Testament at Garrett-Evangelical Theological Seminary.

Presian R. Burroughs, Th.D. is an adjunct professor at Duke Divinity School, a New Testament scholar, researcher, writer, and a United Methodist layperson.

Stephen Riley, Ph.D. is the Director of Academic Assessment at the University of Denver.

Charles Rivera, Ph.D. is an Assistant Professor of Church History at Wake Forest University School of Divinity.

Diana Abernethy, Ph.D. is an Assistant Professor of Religion at Huntingdon College.

Kristin Helms, Ph.D. is an Associate Professor of Biblical Studies and the Academic Director for the Department of Religion and Philosophy at Roberts Wesleyan University.

Jennifer S. Wyant, Ph.D. is the Executive and Teaching Pastor at Johns Creek United Methodist Church and an adjunct instructor for Candler School of Theology at Emory University and teaches for their Course of Study program.

Introduction

Frederick David Carr and Brady Alan Beard

What is *Wesleyan* about Wesleyan biblical interpretation? This book offers some answers to that timely question in the form of short essays, completed with John Wesley's writings in one hand and the Bible in the other. We are, to be sure, not the first to ask this sort of question, and none of this work's contributors would claim to give, or even possess, *the* definitive answer. Rather, each chapter contributes a piece to the larger mosaic of Wesleyan scriptural readings by discussing some aspect of Wesleyan interpretation and its relevance for contemporary Christians. Moreover, these discussions provide some fresh starting points for future explorations into how those within Wesleyan Christianity can interpret the Bible in ways that are faithful to our theological heritage. This collection is, therefore, part of a longer theological journey, and it contributes resources to future expeditions.

The Nature of the Journey

Before embarking on this task, it will be helpful to unpack the guiding question that we ask above. First, what do we mean by *Wesleyan* biblical interpretation? We can begin by answering in the negative: we do not refer to interpretation in or for a specific denomination. We use the term broadly to refer to North American church traditions that trace their origins to the Methodist movement founded by John and Charles Wesley. These traditions persist in numerous denominations, which include but are not limited to, The United Methodist Church, the African Methodist Episcopal Church, the Christian Methodist Episcopal Church, and holiness traditions such as the Free

Methodist Church, the Wesleyan Church, the Church of God (Anderson), and others. Put simply, this book is intended for all who understand themselves, however broadly, to be participants in the larger Wesleyan tradition.

Next, what do we mean by Wesleyan *biblical interpretation*? Here again, we begin with what we do not have in mind, namely, a narrow definition for what counts as "correct" biblical interpretation in general or Wesleyan biblical interpretation in particular. The church has practiced diverse ways of reading Scripture throughout its history, and there are numerous, legitimate ways to engage the biblical texts. For the purposes of this book, we focus on ways of interpreting the Bible with concern for the Wesleyan/Methodist church's theology, doctrine, and practice. Thus, our question could be restated as follows: *What is distinctive about how Wesleyans read the Bible for the church?* Although we ask this question sincerely and openly, the chapters that follow build on two fundamental convictions concerning Wesleyan biblical interpretation, and these convictions give shape to the work as a whole.

First, we hold as foundational that biblical interpretation in the Wesleyan tradition is characterized by what is commonly referred to as "practical divinity." More specifically, those within Methodism interpret Scripture in ways that inform the contemporary church's *praxis*—its life, ministries, and mission. This book, then, in both its structure and its content, reflects the conviction that Wesleyan readings of Scripture, in their varied emphases and forms, should serve the needs of the contemporary church. This assumption emerges ultimately from John Wesley's understanding of holiness: if anything makes Wesleyans Wesleyan, it is our commitment to the church's holiness, understood as a process from justification, through sanctification, and on to perfection in love, all of which are enabled and empowered by God's grace. This theological and practical commitment governs Wesleyan identity, theology, and practice, including practices of biblical interpretation. Thus, to borrow language from The United Methodist Church's mission statement, we hold as a starting point that Wesleyan biblical theology is a part of our call to become and "make disciples of Jesus Christ for the transformation of the world."

Biblical interpretation as an exercise in practical divinity is not unique to Methodism, but it is a distinctively Wesleyan approach to biblical study. Moreover, it is also an urgent and vital topic for Wesleyan Christians to consider in our historical context. As we write this introduction, Methodist traditions are splintering, and new movements are emerging in response. The United States is currently characterized by extreme ideological and political polarization, historic income inequality, the persistence of discrimination against marginalized people, a rise in racially and ethnically motivated hate crimes, increased rates of mental illness and suicide, controversies over immigration, unpredictable futures due to ongoing international military conflicts, the realities of global climate change, and more. Regardless of the near-term results of denominational decisions, local and national elections, law changes, or reform movements, the evidence points overwhelmingly to a long-term need for Christians to reflect deeply on what it means for them to interpret the Bible in ways that can provide theological resources for the church in tumultuous times. This book explores ways that those in the Wesleyan tradition can interpret the Bible in and for its diverse churches.

The second fundamental conviction upon which this work builds is that Wesleyan biblical interpretation is decidedly non-systematic in its expression, largely because it is done for the varied and sometimes unpredictable needs of the church. This is not to say that it is inconsistent, incoherent, or not well thought through. What we mean is that when we search for the "raw materials" from our history from which we can discern the nature of Wesleyan biblical interpretation, we do not find from John or Charles Wesley a sustained theological treatise—or even a full-length book—on the topic. What we find instead is a disparate collection of occasional writings in which the Bible is studied, interpreted, and put to use for specific concerns. These writings do not resemble major, systematic tomes like Thomas Aquinas's *Summa Theologica* or John Calvin's *Institutes of the Christian Religion*. Rather, they come down to us in expressions of scriptural interpretation in the form of Wesley's "notes" on the full Bible, as well as his sermons, liturgies, study notes, journals, tracts, and more.

Is this non-systematic approach to biblical interpretation a problem for the church? Far from it! In much the same way that the Psalms and Paul's letters emerged as focused and context-specific writings, we in the Wesleyan tradition benefit from an array of models for biblical interpretation that were developed "on the ground" in the early Methodist movement. We suggest that this non-systematic approach is not only a strength but also a defining characteristic of Wesleyan biblical interpretation. The shape of this volume, as a collection of distinct and focused forays into the Bible, reflects that conviction.

Finally, to consider how Wesleyans read the Bible for the church, some comments on the nature of interpretation—more formally called hermeneutics—are in order. If the past century or so has taught us anything, it's that we cannot presume to interpret the Bible, or anything else, from a place of pure objectivity. Instead, we bring our backgrounds, experiences, perspectives, biases, presuppositions, and tendencies to the texts, and all of these inevitably influence our interpretations. If that's true in general, then readers within Wesleyan Christianity must do the hard work of examining how our Wesleyan traditions have and might influence our biblical interpretation, as well as to what ends we interpret. A key challenge to those tasks, however, is that it's very difficult to account for our own interpretive lenses and how they influence our readings. Our interpretive biases often remain hidden from us, and the ends to which we read Scripture frequently remain implicit. Nevertheless, these points reflect at least one way in which the essays in this volume practice Methodist interpretation: all of the authors have been formed by the theologies and practices of Wesleyan Christianity, and that formation has contributed to their interpretive sensibilities.

A second feature of interpretation has to do with intentionally designed interpretive models. Over the past half century or so, scholars have developed a number of interpretive frameworks that serve to guide interpretations towards certain ends. These include, for example, feminist, womanist, African American, Latinx, Asian, ecological, and ecclesial interpretive models. A presupposition of such models is that the Bible can be interpreted in diverse ways and, at times, it is necessary to develop interpretive approaches that serve specific communities and moral or theological needs. Many of the essays in this volume also work in this direction: they explore what some of the key reference points for Wesleyan biblical interpretation might include.

We can't presume to read the Bible as investigators in search of meaning somewhere out there waiting to be discovered. Rather, we bring ourselves to the texts, and the process of reading *produces* meaning as interpreters from diverse contexts encounter the biblical writings. The authors of this volume

Introduction

consider how Wesleyan interpretive lenses can produce meaning for Wesleyan Christians.

A Road Map

A distinctive feature of this volume is that we have asked our authors, as much as possible, to interpret biblical texts in their chapters. Although there are several volumes that either explore the contours of Wesleyan biblical interpretation in the abstract or that feature interpretations of the Bible from Methodist perspectives, this collection aims to do both. Moreover, the authors of the chapters that follow each write as longtime participants in Wesleyan Christianity, and their essays demonstrate their commitments to the two foundational convictions discussed above. Each discusses some aspect of what is Wesleyan about Wesleyan biblical interpretation in conversation with one or more of John Wesley's writings. Furthermore, most of the chapters engage, with varying degrees of depth, scriptural texts to showcase some aspect of Wesleyan biblical interpretation with attention to needs of the contemporary church. In this way, each chapter serves as a particular model of, and a focused exploration in, the practice of Wesleyan biblical interpretation for others to learn from and build on in their lives and ministries.

In the first chapter Rob Wall draws together a career's worth of insights to offer an introductory overview of Wesleyan biblical interpretation. Although one could read the chapters in this book in any order, Wall's chapter frames the volume in many ways and provides a logical entry point into the topic. In chapter 2, Cheryl Anderson employs a Wesleyan biblical hermeneutic to address the HIV and AIDS pandemic. She argues that the influence of the Prosperity Gospel has hindered ecclesial discussions and efforts for HIV prevention, and she draws on insights from Wesleyan biblical interpretation to offer alternative theological perspectives on the pandemic. Presian Burroughs uses chapter 3 to examine what she calls "Wesley's ecological approach to interpretation," and, after employing this Wesleyan approach to Romans 8:19-22, she contributes theological perspectives on contemporary ecological practices within the church and offers some reflections on what they suggest for future discussions. In chapter 4, Stephen Riley discusses the Book of Judges, with particular focus on the character of Samson, and highlights how it, along with other Old Testament writings, can play important roles in Wesleyan practices of self-examination and repentance as part of one's commitments to living a holy life. In chapter 5, Charles Rivera highlights the Wesleyan practice of drawing on historical Christian traditions to aid biblical interpretation, and he tackles the difficult question of how Scripture can portray God as both loving and wrathful in conversation with the works of patristic writers, in particular Origen and Ephrem. In chapter 6, Diana Abernathy explores John Wesley's methods for interpreting the Old Testament (OT) in conversation with the best biblical scholarship of his day. After reading Numbers 21:4-9 under the guidance of Wesley's model, she discusses several implications of this methodology for contemporary Christians. In chapter 7, Kristin Helms discusses Wesley's use of philosophy in his theological reflections to address the problem and inevitability of differing biblical interpretations. In particular, she examines Exodus 2:1-10 in conversation with an area of philosophical study known as conceptual metaphor theory to offer constructive guides for contemporary readers. Finally in the eighth chapter, Jennifer Wyant uses John Wesley's method for reading troubling passages in the Bible, and she uses it to interpret Jesus's challenging language in Matthew 15:21-28 as a model for how Wesleyans can work with difficult texts.

Although this volume's contributors are all credentialed scholars, our primary audience is not the academy. We hope, of course, that these essays will benefit academics who have personal or professional interests in Wesleyan hermeneutics. Yet we write mainly for practitioners and students within Wesleyan traditions. As editors, our initial desire to complete this project arose from our experiences of teaching Course of Study classes for The UMC—experiences that revealed to us a need for more resources to help learners understand what it means to interpret the Bible as Methodist/Wesleyan Christians. We therefore hope that this collection will edify clergy, varieties of learners (e.g., in colleges, seminaries, ecclesial programs, small groups) for whom the subject matter is important.

In short, this volume explores the ways that Wesleyan interpretation of Scripture can function as a means of grace that informs the beliefs and meets the needs of Wesleyan Christians. In the pages of Scripture, we expect to find the "word of the Living God" (Wesley, *Explanatory Notes Upon the New Testament*, 5) and to experience the mediation of divine grace. We hope that this collection aids readers as they experience that grace in their practices of interpreting Scripture.

References

Wesley, John, 1986. *Explanatory Notes Upon the New Testament.* 2 vols. Reprint. Peabody, MA: Hendrickson.

For Further Reading

Robert D. Branson, ed. 2020. *Global Wesleyan Encyclopedia of Biblical Theology.* Kansas City: The Foundry Publishing.

Collins, Kenneth J., and Robert W. Wall, eds. 2020. *Wesley One Volume Commentary.* Nashville: Abingdon Press.

Green, Joel B. 2010. *Reading Scripture as Wesleyans.* Nashville: Abingdon Press.

Green, Joel B., and David F. Watson. 2012. *Wesley, Wesleyans, and Reading Bible as Scripture.* Waco: Baylor University Press.

Lancaster, Sarah Heaner. 2011. "Scripture and Revelation." In *The Oxford Handbook of Methodist Studies*, edited by James E. Kirby and William J. Abraham, 489–504. Oxford: Oxford University Press.

Leclerc, Diane. 2001. "Wesleyan-Holiness-Feminist Hermeneutics: Historical Rendering, Current Considerations: Wesleyan Theological Journal." *Wesleyan Theological Journal* 36, no. 2: 105–32.

Maddox, Randy. 2011. The Rule of Christian Faith, Practice, and Hope: John Wesley on the Bible," *Methodist Review* 3: 2–12.

A Commentary in the Wesleyan Tradition. New Beacon Commentaries. 2008–2021. Kansas City, MO: Beacon Hill Press.

Pak, G. Sujin. 2021. "John Wesley and the Protestant Reformers on Scripture." In *Thy Grace Restore, Thy Work Revive: Revival, Reform, and Revolution in Global Methodism.* Essays from the 14th Oxford Institute of Methodist Theological Studies, edited by Sarah Heaner Lancaster, 16–29. Nashville: Wesley's Foundery Books.

Shelton, Raymond Larry, and David R. Wilson. 2013. "Wesleyan Biblical Interpretation." In *The Oxford Encyclopedia of Biblical Interpretation*, 2 vols., edited by Steven L. McKenzie, 2:437–48. Oxford: Oxford University Press.

CHAPTER 1
"The Way of Full Salvation"
An Introduction to Wesleyan Biblical Interpretation[1]

Robert W. Wall

What makes Wesleyan Bible study similar to yet distinct from Wesley's practice of reading Scripture for his day? This fundamental question undergirds this collection of essays. The question also presumes what a distinctively Wesleyan approach to biblical interpretation is not: it does not simply parrot or parade Wesley's notes on biblical texts as the normative Wesleyan reading once for all time. An honest, updated assessment of Wesley's performances of Scripture sometimes prove him wrong. In any case, let me offer—provisionally so—a brief response to this guiding question.

The distinction between "Wesley" and "Wesleyan" implicates methodological differences. To speak of Wesley's interpretation of Scripture requires an investigation of the key sources of his Bible practice—his sermons, his *Explanatory Notes Upon the Old Testament,* his *Explanatory Notes Upon the New Testament,* his journal, and so on—within the bounds of the social

---

1. Much of the present essay is an edited compilation of bits from several of my earlier studies of Wesley's conception and practice of Scripture including: Wall 1999, Wall 2004a; Wall 2004b; Wall 2009; Wall 2011; and especially Wall 2012. A more general account of a theology of Scripture and its practice, which depends upon a Wesleyan theological understanding of Scripture—its nature and practices—as a Spirit-directed means of grace, is now found in Castelo and Wall 2019.

world that shaped them. The method of doing that work follows the rules of modern historical research. Its endgame is to describe fairly and carefully the social and religious world of the eighteenth century in which we might better understand the hows and whys of Wesley's use of biblical texts.

The method advanced in this volume is theological in nature. That is, while interested in how Wesley interpreted biblical texts, a Wesleyan reading of Scripture is primarily interested in retrieving a "Wesleyan sense" from a studied text in ways that help all believers, especially Methodists, form covenant-keeping responses to the challenges they face today. In this way, the reception and exegesis of Scripture by and for contemporary Methodists will continue along the same theological arc of Wesley's biblical account of God's "way of full salvation." What regulates or guides Wesleyan biblical interpretation, then, is not Wesley's particular reading of biblical texts but rather his theological vision of God's promised salvation from the guilt and power of sin worked out in the full transformation of human existence, which a Wesleyan understands in both personal/relational and systemic/societal terms.

Although it is reasonable to expect that a Wesleyan interpretation of Scripture will bear a striking family resemblance to the interests and ends of Wesley's own Bible practices and commentary, we should, as with any "living tradition," expect fresh interpretations that are prompted by ever-changing ecclesial and social landscapes. The history of the Bible's interpretation, in both the East and West, makes it very clear that no one size fits all. In fact, those historians who seek to understand Wesley in his own world note that his engagement with and use of Scripture in his sermons mark out different stages of his theological development: Wesley maintained certain fixed beliefs and practices through a lifetime of ministry, but also progressed in his understanding of God's way of full salvation continually, making adjustments in response to new challenges, questions, problems, and settings that Wesley encountered during a long and fruitful ministry of the gospel.

Whatever else it is, Wesleyan biblical interpretation certainly requires more than an individual's membership in a self-aware congregation with a Methodist lineage—although this certainly helps. It even requires more than bringing an informed understanding of Wesleyan theology to the interpretive task—although this helps as well. More than any other practice, interpreters who are self-critically aware of Wesley's "way of salvation" (*via salutis*) will regulate their theological interpretation and instruction of Scripture to elaborate the core beliefs and practices of our tradition. Yes, there are different ways of doing this, mostly due to differences in interpretative strategies, social locations, personality, and thematic interests. What all Wesleyan biblical interpretation has in common is a profound desire to bring a Wesleyan sense of Scripture's witness to God and God's way of salvation to biblical interpretation in ways that form Christians drenched in what Albert Outler called a "Wesleyan spirit:" a people whose confessional differences and holy love especially for the last, lost, and least are widely known as "Wesleyan."

Bible Study in and for the Church

Before we explore the contours of Wesley's and Wesleyan biblical interpretation, we should first consider the study of the Bible more generally. Serious students read and study the Bible for various reasons and to different ends. Most do so as an act of devotion to God with confidence that the church's Scripture is God's word for God's people. They do so because disciplined Bible study supplies a practical vision for ordering their lives and relationships according to the ways of a holy and loving God.

No one should assume, however, that Scripture's role in forming a covenant-keeping people happens easily or without the guidance of others. Our primary guide is the Holy Spirit who shepherds believers into all truth (John 16:13) and does so by calling to mind the words and deeds of Jesus, God's word personified (John 13:26; cf. 1:1-8). One way God's Spirit accomplishes this illuminating work is through our partnering with informed and skillful teachers who guide close readings of Scripture that target a clear understanding and experience of God's full salvation. Along with the Ethiopian eunuch in Acts 8, receptive students recognize that it is often hard to understand Scripture without someone to teach them. Thus, trusted teachers aspire to play the role of Philip in Acts 8—to explain texts expertly, in ways that make their witness to Jesus more manifest to expectant readers.

Many of the guiding resources students typically use today separate a historically informed interpretation of biblical texts from those theological, moral, and pastoral applications that animate the imaginations of most believers. This division of labor reflects a pattern of theological education typically found in the church-related academy, which separates Bible study from these more practical concerns, such as what Scripture teaches us about God, about God's vision for human life, and about our relations with all others. Scripture is God's gift to God's people that helps them navigate their way through the messy, sin-infested world in which we live. Firm belief, constant prayer, and disciplined practice that form a deeper love of God and neighbor: these are the holy ends of biblical interpretation for Christians.

Let me add two important "footnotes" that anticipate my discussion of Wesleyan theological interpretation of Scripture below. First, Bible study that routinely participates in God's way of full salvation most often occurs in classrooms or congregations that purposely cultivate those inward dispositions necessary for a careful reading of *sacred* texts—that is, texts selected and sanctified by the Holy Spirit to form a people belonging to God. Wesley describes the new birth of this people as a "vast change" monitored and mediated by God's Spirit that imparts new capacities in discerning right from wrong, truth from falsehood. Most of these dispositions are conveniently catalogued throughout Scripture as "fruit of the Spirit" (Gal. 5:22-23), for example, or as "wisdom from above" (James 3:17). Four dispositions, and the practices they embody, are especially worth noting as relevant for the hard work of interpreting Scripture in ways that shape our worship of God and deeper love for God and neighbor.

(1) *Truth-questing*. Students on a quest for God's word in Scripture must engage in an honest interrogation of the meaning and relevance of biblical texts for today's world. While 1 John 2:20-27 speaks of a charismatic experience ("anointing") that enables believers to know God's truth when they hear it—a word that rings true without being taught it in writing or speech—James exhorts readers to receive God's word by closely reading what Scripture says, not in a self-deceptive way but as though one "gazes into" Scripture as one does when looking into a mirror to find there who they truly are (cf. James 1:22-24). So, while the Spirit forms this deep desire within believers to seek truth and even a sense of what kind of truth to seek, the search for truth is often realized by a close reading of God's word in Scripture. Interpretative

errors are often the result of not paying close attention to all the available evidence that may either confirm or reject a presumption of what the text actually says. Honesty and humility are the watchwords of careful Bible study.

(2) *Hospitality*. Biblical interpretation is a community's practice. Recent studies of Paul's use of Scripture have shown that the biblical texts he used to secure his gospel's claims about Jesus were often the very same texts studied by other Jewish teachers (rabbis) of his day. In effect, Paul participated in a community of interpretation that read the same Bible as Scripture, but he read it differently than the others because of the different experiences and beliefs forged by his relationship with the risen Messiah. Nonetheless, what seems clear to Bible scholars is that Paul's use of the Scriptures was shaped by his conversations with other Jewish teachers. Another practice of effective Bible study, then, is to welcome and give seats to a variety of interpreters for a constructive conversation.

(3) *Patience*. Scripture repeatedly exhorts its readers to cultivate the virtue of patience. Often some future goal is given as good reason to be patient. For example, 2 Peter writes that God's patience is motivated by God's desire to give all people time and opportunity to "come to repentance" (2 Pet. 3:9). Gospel stories that remember Jesus's patience in the face of the hostility and suffering he experienced are cued, according to John's Gospel, by his awareness that his hour had not yet come (John 2:4; 7:30; 8:20); more time was needed for him to complete his messianic mission. Sufficient time is necessary in Bible study as well so that students have the time necessary to seek out and discover the full meaning of biblical texts. It takes time to learn, to grow into God's love.

(4) *Forgiveness*. We are all aware that Bible study frequently provokes disagreements and divisions between earnest Christians. Often a divided opinion over the meaning of difficult texts or how Scripture speaks into today's complex social issues is the result of real differences between readers—their beliefs, interpretive methods, experiences, politics, social class, gender, education, and so on. A forgiving disposition embraces a community's diversity with a critical awareness and a deep desire to engage others in animated dialogue in ways that seek to build up rather than tear down the body of Christ. This requires a readiness of every conversation partner to forgive and be forgiven of the tendency to "other" those who disagree with us and to

cultivate the Spirit-led capacity to discuss and debate Scripture so that our study together "building up the body of Christ until we all attain the unity of the faith and knowledge of God's Son" (Eph. 4:12-13 CEB).

My second "footnote" attends more directly to the purpose of this book: the practice of reading Scripture among and for "a people called Methodist." This collection of essays intends to guide readers who seek after the "Wesleyan sense" of Scripture for use in their worship, instruction, mission, and personal devotions. One of the practical reasons typically offered in defense of modern critical approaches to biblical studies is that it helps rid interpretation of a confessional bias, both explicit and implicit. This modern idea of neutrality is demonstrably impossible to maintain in practice: every reader comes to Scripture with a bone to pick, shaped as we all are by deeply personal experiences in our social and religious locations. Moreover, if we approach the Bible as a people of faith, then we will seek out goods in our study that animate our worship of God in those particular settings where the formation of a robust Christian faith is front-and-center. In fact, Scripture's primary residence is the church. The questions Christians rightly ask Scripture are biased toward the formation of their faith in and love for God: What is God's word in this text? How does this text speak to today's front-page news? If the goal of biblical interpretation is to know God and to form a satisfying relationship with God, then the questions we ask of the biblical texts we study are theological in content and practical in consequence.

This quest of the "Wesleyan sense" of Scripture, then, is earthed in trust rather than doubt or dispute with others. A central purpose of providing this resource is to help its readers become more fluent in a Wesleyan theological reading of Scripture for worship, instruction, mission, and personal devotions, all of which make a distinctively Wesleyan contribution to Christ's entire church. The intention is not sectarian or divisive but rather to make clearer the particular contribution of the Wesleyan communion of saints for one holy catholic and apostolic church. The history of using Scripture, whether in the church, the modern academy, or the public square, clearly shows that any biblical story is capable of multiple interpretations; not every interpretation, however, retrieves a Wesleyan sense of Scripture or its intended result: a robust experience of God's full salvation to which one testifies as evidence of

God's promise of new birth. The holy end of targeting this redemptive effect is not to renew a sectarian interest in the Methodist tradition but to form a deeper commitment to its legacy in order to participate more fully and confidently as Wesleyans in the ecumenical conversation of the contemporary global church.

Wesley's Interpretation of Scripture

To appeal to John Wesley as exemplary in matters of biblical interpretation is a no-brainer, at least to Methodists! Although he never wrote a treatise or preached a sermon that examined his core affirmations about Scripture, he famously called himself "a man of one book." (*Preface to The Sermons on Several Occasions*, ¶5). What he meant is that the Bible was his go-to text for Christian discipleship—the indispensable instrument of the Spirit's formative work in congregational worship and mission, instruction, and personal devotions.

There is no clearer expression of Wesley's aim for Scripture's faithful reader than that found in the added prefatory sentence that gives instructions "To the Reader" of his edited version of Thomas Cranmer's *Homilies*: "He that desires to more perfectly understand these great doctrines of Christianity (i.e., salvation, faith and good works) ought diligently to read the Holy Scriptures, especially St. Paul's Epistles to the Romans and the Galatians" (Outler 1964, 123; Wall 2010, 118–22). While this sentiment is widely shared by Protestants even today, Wesley reads Scripture from and for a particular social location at a pivotal moment and in a crucial place in the history of the Christian Bible—eighteenth-century England when the study of Scripture, forged in the fires of the Magisterial Reformation, was reshaped by England's reception of the Enlightenment. Wesley's Bible practices were steeped in both the Protestant principle of *sola scriptura* and the epistemology of scientific humanism, which prompted him to practice the earliest tools of modern biblical criticism but in service of the church to the glory of God.

Whether in the teahouses of London or the classrooms of Oxford and Cambridge, England's reception of the Enlightenment concerned human nature and the nature of divine revelation. Central to the hard, intellectual battles occasioned by this interplay of the human (especially free will) and divine was the rejection of *mere* religious tradition, insisting that any claim for revealed truth must be held accountable to human reason and experience. Wesley agreed and worked hard to construct firm supports for his theology. He selectively admired the work of John Locke, whose philosophy of sense perception (empiricism) promised that any person could and should apply scientific reasoning to what they learned from personal experience (Howcroft 1998, 28–42). That is, a close and honest observation of an experienced life is foundational for understanding human nature and a certain kind of evidence based on divine revelation. Such an idea seemed to agree with the apologetics of the great Renaissance philosopher, Hugo Grotius, who considered competent human testimony, including that found in biblical stories, as solid evidence that helps secure a belief in the very miracles and fulfilled prophecy that validated Scripture's special revelation

Wesley's spiritual reawakening at Aldersgate was a defining moment in his intellectual journey. His religious experience led him to extend his empiricism to include the spiritual senses—that is the sensory experiences of God's grace that forge a more expansive understanding of the real world to include the spiritual world occupied by a transcendent God and marked out by the work and witness of God's Spirit. We learn about God not only by the media of special revelation, such as Scripture, but also by our inward experiences of God's real presence, which confirm and are confirmed by the church's creed and canon.

Wesley received and studied both canon and creed, along with the traditions and histories that attended each, with gratitude and scrupulous attention (Outler 1991, 77). He embraced the Reformation's emphasis on the individual believer's freedom to interpret the Bible, and he was well schooled in Renaissance humanism with its keen interest in the Bible's original languages and sources. Wesley embraced the critical methods of his day, including a lifelong interest in textual translation and literary criticism, and the importance of reading sacred texts in their linguistic and historical contexts. While he firmly rejected David Hume's turn toward religious skepticism, he famously responded to those who accused him (and Methodism) of uncritical "enthusiasm" (or even of sectarian "fanaticism") that "to renounce reason is to renounce religion . . . and that all irrational religion is false religion" (Letter to Dr. Rutherforth 1768, *Works* 9:382; Maddox 2011, 5–7).

England's reception of the Enlightenment continued the values of Renaissance humanism, emphasizing in particular the inherent worth and social progress of each individual. This emphasis also shaped Wesley's interpretive interests (Dawes 2003, 1–10). He baptized the grand ideal of Enlightenment thought that every person should pursue personal happiness by his emphasis on holiness (the holy person is the happy person) and the transforming power of divine love that cooperates with the believer's obedience in reforming grace-filled believers according to the likeness of Christ. Yet this optimism in an individual's potential for life, liberty, and happiness was chastened by the Evangelical Revival of the 1730s and its reminder of a person's inability to flourish in the face of persistent sin without a radical intervention of divine grace. While David Bebbington reminds us that this great Revival, in which Wesley played a significant role, carried a theological freight keenly influenced by the optimistic tempers of England's Enlightenment, Aldersgate taught Wesley that the way forward toward human flourishing is predicated on an "optimism of grace" (Bebbington 1989, 50–66). Reading Scripture without doubt and in firm confidence of God's good company is an essential marker of Wesley's hermeneutics, whether applied to his morning office or in sermon preparation for his congregation.

In fact, Wesley's congregation included many unschooled rank-and-file converts, who were deeply interested in Scripture's teaching. Despite their limitations on education, most of his congregants could detect obscure biblical allusions in current popular literature. Biblical commentaries topped the list of books borrowed from the public libraries and purchase of inexpensive Bible study aids quadrupled the sales of any other kind of publication (Preston 1982, 98–102). Wesley himself contributed to this robust market of ordinary readers by publishing his best-selling *Explanatory Notes*. Wesley's interpretation of Scripture was not only responsive to a widespread cultural interest in Bible study, but was also engaged with a particular audience that saw him as their spiritual director. Perhaps for this reason, he rarely mentions the contemporary controversies of the educated elites, not because he thought them impious or unimportant, but for fear that to "inflame the hearts of

Christians against each other" might distract his readers from hearing "the Master's word, to imbibe his Spirit, and to transcribe his life into our own" (*NT Notes*, §9).

Most of Wesley's sermons include long strings of different Bible verses cobbled together, one interpreting the other. He writes to John Newton, that "The Bible is my standard of language as well as sentiment. I endeavor not only to think but *to speak* as the oracles of God" (Letter to John Newton April 1, 1766, *Works* 28:12). Wesley sometimes expresses concern for a preacher's orthodoxy when hearing a sermon that did not contain much quoted Scripture. His concern is not simply rhetorical but theological: quoting Scripture is a matter of trusting Scripture. If the very nature of Scripture is holy and its effect produces salvation, then its words read aloud can disclose God without need of the preacher's pretentious adornments.

Wesley's Theological Perspectives on Scripture

We can retrieve a broad outline of Wesley's theology of Scripture from the Prefaces to his *Explanatory Notes Upon the New Testament* (1754) and *Explanatory Notes Upon the Old Testament* (1765). Central to his approach to Scripture is that readers approach the holy text to "observe the word of the living God . . . which remaineth forever" (*NT Notes*, §10). Scripture is not the depository of timeless truth-claims to be asserted in theological discourse, but a "fountain of heavenly wisdom" that is "tasted as good" because it helps construct a holy space into which a congregation of the faithful enters to meet with the Spirit to hear again in Scripture the words of a living God (*NT Notes*, §10). This holy wisdom is hardly outdated, since God's words are "of inexhaustible virtue" (*NT Notes*, §12). The human language and genre of the biblical texts we study "sink nothing before it (since) God speaks not as man but as God." Scripture is "a grammar of the language of the Holy Ghost" (*NT Notes*, §12). Scripture thus proceeds from God by the action of the sanctifying Spirit who graciously illumines the community of hearers who understand it as God's instruction and as a means of God's saving grace. As such, Scripture's interpretation must aim to give its audience "the direct, literal meaning of every verse, of every sentence, and as far as I am able of every word in the oracles of God" (*OT Notes*, §15). This is not to say that Wesley read Scripture "literally" in the sense that contemporary readers might. Rather, he read it carefully to seek what the text plainly says, a text sanctified by the Holy Spirit to guide the church continually in the ways of God.[2]

In Wesley's influential work, "An Address to the Clergy" (1756), Wesley speaks of the importance of "acquired endowments" (Jackson *Works*, 10:482). Reflective of his Enlightenment era context, Wesley claims that knowledge is first among these skills and then goes on to catalog different kinds of knowledge that clergy must learn. Most important is the minister's knowledge "of all the Scriptures"—*all* the Scriptures since "one part fixes the sense of another." Wesley claims that "none can be a good Divine who is not a good textuary. None else can be mighty in the Scriptures, able both to instruct and to stop the mouths of gainsayers" (Jackson *Works*, 10:482), which surely are the two essential tasks of clergy by his definition.

In explaining what kind of biblical knowledge clergy must acquire, Wesley asks this critical question: "Ought he not to know the literal meaning of every word, verse, and chapter, without which there can be no firm foundation on which the spiritual can be built?" (Jackson *Works*, 10:482). Two observations must frame any discussion of Wesley's definition of Scripture's literal sense. First, his interpretive strategy is text-centered. There is no task more important than the sacred text's address of its faithful, careful reader. Careful Bible study that grounds what we find there in textual, historical, experiential, natural evidences secures the good student's "firm foundation." Second, a "good textuary" is expected to seek after "the spiritual." That is, to hold every word of Scripture allows the reader to gain a sense of the text's theological meaning and practical application. Wesley's typical move is, therefore, from a text's plain sense to its practical applications for spiritual formation.

Wesley's movement from plain sense to spiritual practices suggests that the text's literal meaning points readers to God's plan of salvation, operationalized

---

2. For a list of five interpretive rules that follow from this conception of Scripture, Introduction, in the *Bicentennial Edition of the Works of John Wesley.* (*Works* 1:57–59) Edited by A. C. Outler. Nashville: Abingdon Press, 1984–. What is lacking for his list is a sixth interpretive rule supplied in Sermon 37, "The Nature of Enthusiasm," *Works*, 2:54–55. According to Wesley, the target of Scripture's interpretation is to know the will of God, "which is our sanctification." Below I seek to apply this general rule to define, in Wesley's implied terms, Scripture's "literal sense."

by means of grace. Wesley follows a familiar practice of biblical interpretation inherited from the Reformation that begins with text-centered exegesis that provides the raw materials of a theological interpretation of Scripture, guided by the analogy of faith, which makes "a suitable application to the consciences of his hearers." This movement from Scripture's literal sense—what the text plainly says—to its theological meaning or *Christian* sense—what the text says about God's way of full salvation—orders the flow of Wesley's sermons and helps locate biblical interpretation in and for the church.

Interestingly, this search for a text's literal sense does not reflect the strategies of the earliest interpreters of Scripture whom Wesley so admired. Wesley agreed with his premodern mentors that the meaning we should seek to retrieve from a biblical text is quite literally its "Christian sense." Differences arise concerning the means by which we achieve this end. Modern biblical criticism seeks to reconstruct this sense as a matter of historical fact and typically locates it at the moment of a composition's origins. A biblical text witnesses to what believers understood of God's ways—its "Christian sense"—when texts were written and first read in terms of the author's intended (i.e., a particular) meaning. The Reformers, followed by Wesley, meant something different: literal sense regards the text's *Christian* meaning. It was the sense ordinary believers made of what they heard or read in the words of Scripture, not the sense made of a replacement storyline created by scholars (Childs 1977, 80–95). Thus, the single sense apprehended by faithful readers of Scripture at and for their social and religious locations, which they testify cultivates their friendship with God, may differ from the single sense apprehended by other faithful readers in different time zones, faith traditions, cultural settings, and so on. This idea of a "multifaceted literal sense" is characteristic of Scripture's reception during the Reformation and by its heirs during Wesley's eighteenth century.[3]

I hope this elaboration of Scripture's literal sense helps to contextualize what Wesley calls "the naked Bible," a rubric that derives from the importance

---

3. Although well beyond the scope of this chapter, let me simply observe that a comparison of Jonathan Edwards's explanatory notes on a sample of set texts in his Blank Bible and those in Wesley's *Notes*—along with the notes of other contemporary interpreters—will reflect their different readings of these texts and help secure this point, which otherwise is made with common sense.

the Reformers placed on the biblical text itself—its translation, its linguistic analysis, its literary form and structure—rather than on its historical background or its cultural foreground. Influenced by Isaac Newton's science of critical observation, Wesley demands the interpreter pay close attention to what the text plainly says and the effects its interpretation produces in life. This is not anti-intellectualism or critical naiveté but a commitment to the meaning of words and phrases rooted in his core belief that those words and phrases are revelatory of God (Wall 2010, 123–124; Jones 1995, 114). At the same time, however, he ridiculed "abstract reasoning" that isolated a careful analysis of the text from its implication for real life. Rather, Wesley sought to discern the will of God in the life of believers.

The Goals of Wesley's Biblical Interpretation

In his often-neglected sermon, "The Nature of Enthusiasm" (Sermon 37), Wesley reflects on *how* one makes inquiries into the will of God. Although a radical response to the more individualistic and inward "enthusiasm" (today we might call it "fanaticism") of his day, as we would expect, Wesley advises one to consult "the oracles of God." But his practical concern is not where to locate God's will but, "how shall I know what is the will of God in such and such a particular case?" (*Works* 2:54). His answer is quite extraordinary and not often included in the various lists of Wesley's hermeneutical rules. It does not concern a textual strategy but *an existential outcome.*

Wesley contends that if God's will in every case is sanctification—"that we should be inwardly and outwardly holy"—then "experience tells (the interpreter) what advantages he has in his present state, either for being or doing good; and reason is to show what he certainly or probably will have in the state proposed" (*Works*, 2:55). *That is, one knows whether a biblical interpretation is a right one by considering whether its actual performance produces a result that accords with holiness.* This discernment is not based on one's critical orthodoxy or even the theological orthodoxy of one's interpretation; it is a measurement of what an interpretation produces in life, whether it contributes to inward or outward holiness and so draws the reader into closer communion with a holy God. Simply put, Wesley's search for the literal or

Christian sense of a text targets a meaning that makes a *particular* communion of readers wise for sanctification (Koskie 2014, 88–119).[4]

Finally, the authority Wesley granted the spiritually mature reader of Scripture should not be minimized in this discussion. Although modernity soon came to value a reader's suspicion of the biblical text and to question its capacity to disclose God's truth about the world, Wesley did not. Quite apart from following the standard rules that guide biblical interpretation, as an heir to the importance the Reformation placed on "inner religion," he emphasizes the formation of a reader's holy dispositions by the means of grace. Grace is a countervailing force to suspicion and rather forms faithful readers more receptive to the Spirit's guidance, thereby more knowing of and responsive to the Scripture way of salvation.

Toward a Wesleyan Theological Interpretation of Scripture

For all the care Wesley took to translate the biblical text accurately, drawing upon his library of trusted experts and his personal and pastoral experiences, Wesley's *Explanatory Note* on Romans 12:6 suggests that the most important constraint in guiding his theological interpretation of Scripture is the church's "analogy of faith." He writes,

> Having then gifts differing according to the grace which is given us - Gifts are various: grace is one. Whether it be prophecy—This, considered as an extraordinary gift, is that whereby heavenly mysteries are declared to men, or things to come foretold. But it seems here to mean the ordinary gift of expounding Scripture. 'Let us prophesy according to the analogy of faith'— St. Peter expresses it, 'as the oracles of God,' according to the general tenor of them, according to that grand scheme of doctrine which is delivered

---

4. My definition assumes that the nature of God who addresses readers in Scripture is living and present (Deut. 5:26; Matt 16:16; 1 Tim. 3:15) and whose self-communication via Scripture's "literal sense" is therefore more particular to the audience and so dynamic and multivoiced in substance and effect. The better way of testing this thesis is to compare different Wesley sermons based upon the same set text but preached or written for different audiences and at different stages of his life—a set text, e.g., such as Ephesians 2:8–10 or John 3:8, among Wesley's most strategic. My findings from a cursory analysis are more in line with Fowl's (2006) idea of a "multivoiced literal sense" for ever-changing audiences than a more static meaning based upon an unchanging theological grammar.

therein, touching original sin, justification by faith, and present, inward salvation. There is a wonderful analogy between all these; and a close and intimate connexion between the chief heads of that faith 'which was once delivered to the saints.' Every article therefore concerning which there is any question should be determined by this rule; every doubtful Scripture interpreted according to the grand truths which run through the whole.

Significantly, Wesley does not take the prophetic gift in its "extraordinary" sense—to declare divine revelation or foretell the future—but in its more mundane sense to "expound Scripture." Perhaps Wesley rightly senses here Paul's exhortation for humility and solidarity. In any case, prophecy is the only gift that Paul links to "the faith": the proper exercise of prophecy—or "expounding Scripture" in Wesley's reading—is "according to the analogy of faith." Wesley takes this phrase as a reference to the apostolic tradition—that is, "the chief heads of the faith 'which was once delivered to the saints.'"

His explanatory note on Paul's use of "the faith" recalls his earlier phrase, "measure of the faith" (Rom. 12:3 KJV), which stipulates a standard of self-criticism: almost certainly Paul does not mean that every believer is given a different "measure" or amount of faith by God but rather that the quotient of Christian faith is equally measured for all believers. The repetition of "faith" in verse 6 carries similar theological freight: the prophet's exposition of Scripture, as Wesley understands the prophetic gift, should agree with the Christian faith in both content and effect.

Although the Greek word (*analogia*) translated "analogy" occurs only here in the New Testament, its basic meaning is well-known in Greek philosophy: an "analogy" relates two subjects in right proportion with each other. For Wesley, Paul's phrase, "analogy of the faith" (12:6), stipulates an interpretive principle: every interpretation of Scripture must exist in right proportion to the core beliefs of the Christian faith. Although these core beliefs were first articulated by the second-century apologist, Irenaeus, in arguing against the church's so-called heretics, he traced these beliefs back to the apostles who first witnessed these truths embodied in the Incarnation. These same beliefs are brought forward and are now found and formulated in the standard creeds of the church catholic, such as the Apostles' Creed or the "Articles of Religion" affirmed by Wesley as a priest of the Church of England.

An apostolic "rule of faith" is thus forged that guides a "right handling of the word of truth" (2 Tim. 2:15 Author's Translation). This same apostolic ruler that measured the theological correctness of biblical interpretations from the very beginning, then also guided the church's formation of the Christian Bible—only those texts whose content conformed to this rule of faith were admitted into the Bible—now continues to guide its ongoing reception and interpretation today under the Spirit's direction, in Tertullian's apt phrase as the "governor for interpretation."

Wesley's idea of an "analogy of faith" prompts the pivotal question of this essay: What, then, are the core theological agreements of "a people called Methodist" that "govern" our interpretation and practice of Scripture in worship, instruction, mission, and personal devotions? I would add that such a ruler measures the content of our interpretations and applications of the biblical text, but it should also guide our approach to a biblical text to interpret it. A *Wesleyan* theological interpretation guides what students target in their word studies, their investigation of a text's grammar, their consideration of those ancient worlds behind and contemporary worlds in front of the biblical texts they are asked faithfully and carefully to investigate.

Via Salutis

Wesley himself helps us by charting a "grand scheme of doctrine" that narrates God's way of full salvation that includes: "original sin, justification by faith, and present, inward salvation." I would note that the various articulations of the apostolic rule of faith—and there have been many from antiquity forward to the church's contemporary creeds—retain a narrative shape, a Trinitarian substance, and seek to relate together the core beliefs of Christian discipleship in a way that allows believers to confess and communicate the content of their owned faith in coherent ways to others. Accordingly, then, what we know and believe about a holy and loving God is inseparable from our knowledge of God's Son and Holy Spirit. This knowledge of God is impossible apart from God's revelation witnessed in history: by God's creation of all things, testified to by the prophets, climaxed in and by the life and work of the risen Jesus and the Pentecost of his Spirit, whose work continues in the transformed life and transforming ministry of the one holy catholic and apostolic church, and will be consummated by the Creator's coming triumph at the return of the risen Lord to complete his messianic work. The catholic—meaning universal—and apostolic church's confession and transforming experience of this narrative of God's gospel, deeply rooted in and confirmed by its collective memory, supplies the rule's raw material. The results of biblical interpretation must ever conform to this confession and experience.

Methodists speak with glad hearts of Wesley's *via salutis*—his "way of salvation." This is his extraordinary "grand scheme of doctrine" that unifies Scripture and both regulates and animates a Wesleyan reading and practice of Scripture. While no part of this grand scheme departs from the doctrinal loci of the church's ecumenical creeds, no part is more strategic to Wesley in this "grand scheme" than the experience of a "new birth," and no reading of Scripture can escape its impress. The believer's regeneration is the linchpin that holds together the believer's justification by faith with an experience "present, inward salvation," which then opens the door to the believer's experience of the transforming power of God's sanctifying grace. It is this final work of divine grace plotted by of Wesley's *via salutis*—the entire sanctification or transformation of human existence—that prompts my paraphrase of Wesley's famous rubric: "the way of *full* salvation" ("The Scripture Way of Salvation" [Sermon 43]).

In his sermon, "The Great Privilege of Those That Are Born of God" (Sermon 19), Wesley explains that while justification occurs when sinners trust God to pardon them from the guilt of inherited and past sins, regeneration occurs when that new believer is released from sin's captive power to begin a new life under the direction of the Spirit. New birth involves a *supernatural* change in human nature. If God's justifying grace puts to rights sinners' personal relationship with God, God's regenerating grace transforms the senses of their inmost soul. They become children of God, reborn with God's image with new capacities for a participatory partnership with God. As Wesley put it, new birth occasions a "vast, inward change" (*Works*, 1:432). All the resources necessary to live a holy life are given by God *at our new birth*, "as soon as he is born of God there is a total change in all his particulars—he sees the light of the world, he hears the voice of God, he feels the love of God shed abroad in his heart by God's Spirit. And now he may properly be said to live" ("The New Birth" [Sermon 45], *Works,* 2:193).

When Scripture's testimony to God's saving grace is understood Wesley's way, regeneration marks a gateway into the body of Christ where still other operations of divine grace begin the hard work of sanctification. Precisely because regeneration changes the will, the believer need not willfully sin. Precisely because regeneration transforms the senses, it is now possible to resist evil tempers and thoughts. Precisely because regeneration restores the image of a loving, truth-telling God within the believer, the believer is now assured of God's love and confident of participating in God's coming victory. Precisely because regeneration purifies the human spirit, God's Spirit can bear witness in our spirit, which in Wesley's understanding paves the path for a robust cooperation between God's people and God's Spirit as broker of God's sanctifying graces.

Central to Wesley's radical conception of Christian existence is this dynamic cooperation between the divine and human spirits that marks out the believer's new birth as God's child (cf. Romans 8). While new birth is a supernatural event that changes our nature, sanctification envisages an unfolding process during which God sanctifies the faithful believer in proportion to the amount and quality of grace received. The various practices of Christian discipleship—works of piety and mercy—when complemented by the ordinary means of grace ordained by the church occasion a profuse outpouring of God's salvation-creating grace that transforms the believer into a conspicuous saint. Every meaning and performance of Scripture at its ecclesial location is analogous of this conception of salvation.

Conclusion

In his comment about Scripture's importance in the Preface to his published sermons, Wesley famously writes, "I want to know one thing, the way to heaven: how to land safe on that happy shore. God Himself has condescended to teach the way; for this very end He came from heaven. He hath written it down in a book! O give me that book! At any price, give me the

Book of God! I have it: here is knowledge enough for me" (*Works*, 1:105)! While Wesley's exuberant note of Scripture's endgame is sometimes taken at face value to dismiss him as a biased biblicist, his exhortation to readers of his sermons underscores two important features of the kind of biblical instruction we hope that this volume will underwrite. I understand Scripture's purchase precisely as Wesley understood it: it discloses a pathway to heaven—that is, a sacred place where God's victory over sin and death is realized. Scripture's referent is the Savior of God's creation, the incarnate Word, through whom we are forgiven and by whom we enjoy the presence of his sanctifying Spirit. While each essay of this collection carries the theological freight of a particular people called Methodists for good and ill, we trust that it will be used by teachers and preachers, students and laypersons from every communion of the global church.

Wesley makes it clear by his own practices that there is no shortcut in the hard work required in forming the competent reader of a text with as many moving parts as Scripture. God's inspired instruction is not magically given nor are its redemptive ends magically produced. For our own day, Wesley stands as our mentor and exemplar in this regard: Scripture is the Spirit's auxiliary for growing the church's wisdom; but such is received only by faithful readers who study the sacred text very carefully in expectation of hearing a sanctifying word from the Lord God Almighty.

References

Bebbington, David. 1989. *Evangelicalism in Modern Britain: A History from the 1730s to the 1980s*. Boston: Unwin Hyman.

Castelo, Daniel and Robert W. Wall. 2019. *The Marks of Scripture: Rethinking the Nature of the Bible*. Grand Rapids: Baker.

Childs, Brevard. 1977. "The *Sensus Literalis* of Scripture: An Ancient and Modern Problem." In *Beiträge zur Alttestamentlichen Theologie: Festschrift für Walther Zimmerli zum 70. Geburtstag*. Edited by Herbert Donner, Robert Hanhart, and Rudolf Smend. 80–95. Göttingen: Vandenhoeck & Ruprecht.

Dawes, S. B. 2003. "John Wesley and the Bible." *Proceedings of the Wesley Historical Society* 54, no. 1: 1–10.

Fowl, Stephen E. 2006. "The Importance of a Multivoiced Literal Sense of Scripture." In *Reading Scripture with the Church: Toward a Hermeneutic for Theological Interpretation*. Edited by A.K.M. Adam, Stephen E. Fowl, Kevin J. Vanhoozer, and Francis Watson, 35-50. Grand Rapids: Baker.

Howcroft, K. G. 1998. "Reason, Interpretation and Postmodernism—Is There a Methodist Way of Reading the Bible?" *Epworth Review* 25, no. 3: 28–41.

Jones, Scott J. 1995. *John Wesley's Conception and Use of Scripture*. Nashville: Abingdon Press.

Koskie, Steven Joe, Jr. 2014. *Reading the Way to Heaven: A Wesleyan Theological Hermeneutic of Scripture. Journal of Theological Interpretation Supplement 8*. Winona Lake, IN: Eisenbrauns.

Maddox, Randy. 2011. "The Rule of Christian Faith." *Methodist Review* 3: 1–35.

Outler, Albert C. 1964. *John Wesley*. New York: Oxford University Press.

———. 1991. "The Wesleyan Quadrilateral—in John Wesley." In *Doctrine and Theology in The United Methodist Church*, edited by Thomas A. Langford, 75–88. Nashville: Abingdon Press.

Preston, Thomas R. 1982. "Biblical Criticism, Literature, and the Eighteenth-Century Reader." In *Books and their Readers in Eighteenth-Century England*, edited by Isabel Rivers, 97–126. Leicester, UK: Leicester University Press.

Wall, Robert W. 1999. "The Rule of Faith in Theological Hermeneutics." In *Between Two Horizons: Spanning New Testament Studies & Systematic Theology*, edited by Joel B. Green and Max Turner, 88–107. Grand Rapids: Eerdmans.

———. 2004. "Toward a Wesleyan Hermeneutic of Scripture." In *Reading the Bible in Wesleyan Ways: Some Constructive Proposals*, edited by Barry L. Callen and Richard P. Thompson, 39–55. Kansas City: Beacon Hill.

———. 2004. "Facilitating Scripture's Future Role Among Wesleyans." In *Reading the Bible in Wesleyan Ways: Some Constructive Proposals*, edited by Barry L. Callen and Richard P. Thompson, 107–22. Kansas City: Beacon Hill.

———. 2010. "Wesley as Biblical Interpreter." In *The Cambridge Companion to John Wesley*, edited by Randy L. Maddox and Jason E. Vickers, 113–128. Cambridge: Cambridge University Press.

———. 2011. "John's John: A Wesleyan Theological Reading of 1 John." *Wesleyan Theological Journal* 46 no. 2: 105–41.

———. 2012. "Reading Scripture, the Literal Sense, and the Analogy of Faith." In *Wesley, Wesleyans, and Reading the Bible as Scripture*, edited by Joel B. Green and David F. Watson, 33–46. Waco: Baylor University Press.

Wesley, John. *The Works of John Wesley*, edited by Thomas Jackson. 14 vols. London:1872, Grand Rapids: Zondervan, 1958.

———. 1975. *Explanatory Notes Upon the Old Testament*. London: Schmul Publishers.

———. 1986. *Explanatory Notes Upon the New Testament*. 2 vols. Reprint. Peabody, MA: Hendrickson.

———. 1984–2024. In *The Bicentennial Edition of the Works of John Wesley*, edited by Randy Maddox, et al. 24 vols. Nashville: Abingdon Press.

———. 1794–1802. "Preface." *Sermons on Several Occasions: In Four Volumes*. Philadelphia: J. Crukshank and John Dickins. https://quod.lib.umich.edu/e/evans/N21366.0001.001/1:3?rgn=div1;view=fulltext.

CHAPTER 2

Wesleyan Biblical Interpretation in the Age of AIDS[1]

Cheryl B. Anderson

For more than fifteen years, I have researched how Christians read (or should read) the Bible in the context of the HIV and AIDS pandemic. My work has focused on my own African American community, but I have incorporated insights resulting from experiences with theological and biblical colleagues who are doing comparable work in South Africa and Brazil. Given the decades of activism globally and medical advancements on the Human Immunodeficiency Virus (HIV) that causes the Acquired Immunodeficiency Syndrome (AIDS), it would be reasonable to expect that new infections would be rare; yet in each of these countries, new infections continue to occur at shockingly high rates. Yet HIV is completely preventable, and information about effective prevention measures has been widely disseminated. Nevertheless, there are clearly impediments that limit the ability of all segments of these populations to learn about and adopt effective prevention methods.

---

1. The original version of this essay appeared in Anderson 2018. With the publisher's permission, it has been revised to fit the purposes of the present publication. For detailed, statistical support for claims made—especially in relation to the HIV and AIDS pandemic—I refer readers to the original essay.

In each of these three countries, there is a high percentage of Christians, and there is a strong Methodist presence. The respective Methodist denominations are The United Methodist Church and the historical African American Methodist traditions in the United States, the Methodist Church of Southern Africa in South Africa, and the Igreja Metodista in Brazil. From my research, I know that each denomination has acted on the AIDS pandemic and has had and continues to have ministries directed toward those who are living with the virus. However, I also know that conversations about effective HIV prevention are rare, that is, ones that would include but go beyond solely promoting abstinence and faithfulness in marriage.

As I have argued elsewhere, the prevention strategy to abstain, be faithful, and, if necessary, use a condom (better known as "ABC"), is not very effective, given contemporary realities (Anderson 2016, 73–92). In the United States, the reluctance to have frank conversations about sexual expression in African American communities has been observed and explained, in part, as a legacy of slavery, where Black sexuality was exploited and demonized (Brown Douglas 1999, 67–86). Another reason, though, is that church leaders and their congregations fear that if they discuss HIV, they would appear to condone behaviors that are associated with its transmission (Cohen 1999; Harris 2010, 5–6). The basic premise of this chapter is that an additional factor hinders church-based discussions and activities around effective HIV prevention, and that factor is the popularity of a brand of theology widely known as the Prosperity Gospel. Essentially, the Prosperity Gospel, or the gospel of "health and wealth," asserts that its faithful believers will receive blessings from God.

My purpose here is to question the use of the Prosperity Gospel by Methodist churches for two reasons. The first reason is that the Prosperity Gospel is not consistent with some basic teachings of John Wesley (1703–1791), the founder of Methodism. The second reason is that, in the age of AIDS, it hinders the ability of Methodist churches to fight new HIV infections in the most effective manner. Therefore, this chapter will argue that John Wesley's approach to comparable theological and biblical issues remains relevant, counters prosperity messages, and can help us to combat the continued spreading of the virus today. Finally, and critically, this chapter will consider a Wesleyan approach to reading Scripture that will enable Methodist churches to return to their heritage, have a more distinctive identity in today's denominational landscape, and actively engage in the lives of their congregations and surrounding populations as they confront a pandemic.

The Prosperity Gospel: Definitions and Advantages

As Sandra Barnes summarizes in her study on the "health and wealth" messages in Black megachurches: "Prosperity theology boasts the promise of spiritual, physical, and material blessings for those who follow its tenets," or stated another way, "one's righteousness and faithfulness necessitate success." Prosperity theology, then, would contend that negative dynamics such as poverty or illness are due to a person's limited faith or "questionable Christian lifestyle" (Barnes 2013, 50–51). Known also by the slogan "Name It and Claim It," the Prosperity Gospel's lineage can be traced to the Word of Faith movement that began in the second half of the twentieth century. As it is now expressed, the Prosperity Gospel has resonances with Pentecostalism and Evangelicalism (Walton 2014, 1, 10; Mitchem 2007). Some of the best-known ministers within this tradition are Kenneth Hagin Sr., Joel Osteen, Kenneth and Gloria Copeland, and Frederick K. Price. T. D. Jakes is also a Word of Faith pastor, and his tremendous commercial success in television, films, and merchandising has arguably redefined the parameters of Christian ministry.

Globally, the Prosperity Gospel movements—or prosperity theologies—constitute "one of the fastest growing segments of Pentecostalism" (Miller and Yamamori 2007, 175). Aspects of prosperity theologies (Walton 2014, 2) can be found in traditional Pentecostal churches, namely, those that trace their heritage back to the Azuza Street experience, such as the Assemblies of God and the Church of God in Christ (COGIC), but those aspects can also be found through charismatic movements in the Roman Catholic Church, traditional Protestant denominations, and even in a new denomination such as the Igreja Universal do Reino de Deus (Universal Church) that started in Brazil in the late 1970s. Regardless of the specific denominational name, the unifying element of these congregations is "an affinity for prosperity messages" (Attanasi and Yong 2012, 3).

On the whole, the Prosperity Gospel provides a message that is sorely needed in a variety of different national and socioeconomic contexts—and it does provide material benefits. For example, Berge Furre suggests that the Universal Church, founded in Brazil but with ministries around the world, helps those who are on the margins of society to survive. For him, today's globalized economy creates a society "without mercy," and the Universal Church becomes a means of survival—by offering survival strategies—for those who have been marginalized in their own country or in another one due to migration patterns that the globalized economy necessitates (Furre 2006, 48–49). Specifically, prosperity messages offer hope and affirmation to every person, and such affirmation can motivate a person to change her or his circumstances (Miller and Yamamori 2007, 169).

Interestingly, the argument can be made that the Prosperity Gospel is also popular with those who are more privileged and not struggling economically. The idea is that, in the United States, the Prosperity Gospel rose in popularity as a stronger economy enabled more African Americans to accumulate wealth. Arguably, this segment of the population no longer saw themselves as "voiceless" or "victims" who needed to take refuge in the traditional Black church, as had happened during the civil rights movements of the 1960s (McGee 2017, 6–16). With the rising economic prosperity of the 1990s, members of the middle and upper classes needed "to affirm and reinforce [their] economic achievements," and the Prosperity Gospel allowed them "to reinterpret the quest of the American dream as central to Christian experience" (Day 2012, 109). However, during the time that some African Americans were accumulating more wealth, an even bigger number were being pushed into an economic underclass. Here, the logic of the Prosperity Gospel served two purposes: it assuaged the guilt of the more affluent (Barnes 2013, 52), and it explained why some prospered and some did not: the latter lacked faith (Day 2012, 109–110).

The Prosperity Gospel and Its Disadvantages in the Age of AIDS

In 2013, Barnes's work *Live Long and Prosper* was published. It is a major study of Black megachurches and their engagement with poverty and the

AIDS pandemic. Although she found that the majority of pastoral leaders did not fully espouse the Prosperity Gospel, she noted its features in their theological perspectives (Barnes 2013, 67–68). Given the pervasiveness of the Prosperity Gospel, she raises the question: If members think that the Christian believer should have "health and wealth," how would these churches address the persistent poverty and disproportionate rates of HIV infections in the African American community? Would they simply ignore those issues? Fortunately, Barnes found that the churches she studied did address both issues—but they addressed them differently. To explain those differences, she discusses multiple "frames" in which such churches view and respond to the pandemic.

One frame views the pandemic as an issue of sexuality. Those with this perspective condemn same-sex relationships and consider HIV primarily to result from immorality and promiscuity in various forms: homosexuality, drug use, and prostitution. Those who have the disease tend to be blamed for their condition; having HIV is understood "as both a warning and a challenge to the unrighteous to make amends." Nevertheless, some churches with this frame have HIV ministries and believe that, as Christians, they are to "Hate the sin and love the sinner" (Barnes 2013, 104–6).

The next frame addresses the pandemic as a health issue. It is based on the Black church tradition of seeing itself as "a spiritual hospital," as well as on Jesus Christ's model of interacting with the lepers and other outcasts of his day. Because this frame does not focus on sexuality, it allows the churches to have HIV-related ministries and to collaborate with other churches and organizations. Though, it is important to note that a pastor interviewed made it a point to say that the "homosexual lifestyle" was still condemned (Barnes 2013, 113–15).

Third, the poverty frame "associates the pandemic largely with the heterosexual population and the risky behavior stemming from poverty and related challenges." This perspective assumes that the impact of a globalized economy, deindustrialization, and mass incarceration creates a state of emotional impoverishment. That impoverishment leads to behaviors that "put their very lives at risk." Thus, if chronic poverty can be countered, then risky behaviors will decrease (Barnes 2013, 115–17).

The final frame is the prosperity frame. It is used by those who fully embrace the Prosperity Gospel. The emphasis here is not on any specific disease, whether HIV, diabetes, or cancer—but on Christ as a healer and the believer's expectation of receiving miracles. The prosperity frame emphasizes the believer "practicing confessing and tithing" and believing in an omnipotent God who can intervene and bring healing, "despite human frailty and medical reports" (Barnes 2013, 119–22).

Barnes concludes that her research shows the need for "multipronged approaches." Such approaches should be "based on a thorough understanding of specific church profiles," which would help to identify "which church cultural tools should be best implemented to encourage involvement, and when and how." She notes that Black churches are able to have HIV ministries, even if they have ongoing concerns about homosexuality. Consequently, she argues there is no need for the Black church to address the fundamental issues of human sexuality or homosexuality before there can be an effective response, as some pastors contend (Barnes 2013, 181). Unfortunately, the current statistics on the patterns of new HIV infections indicate that those fundamental issues do need to be addressed.

In the United States today, two groups are most disproportionately impacted by HIV, and they are both African American. One is gay men (or "men who have sex with men" [MSM], whether or not they would refer to themselves as homosexual). The other is heterosexual women. Moreover, the inordinate impact on Black women can be observed to an even greater degree in sub-Saharan Africa where, unlike the United States and Brazil, the virus is spread primarily through heterosexual sex. Globally, two groups—gay men and heterosexual women—are excessively affected by the AIDS pandemic, and it is worthwhile to explore why.

Of course, a variety of factors drive the pandemic, but an important one—and the one that negatively affects these two groups—is the traditional gender paradigm. This paradigm presumes a hierarchy of men over women and basically means that men must always be dominant and women must always be subordinate. If men must always be dominant, then homosexuality is condemned, because it would involve a man who is subordinate, that is, in the female position (Fewell and Gunn 1993, 107–8; Martin 2006, 58–59).[2]

In the context of HIV, when homosexuality is condemned, gay men are made more vulnerable to infection. For example, if a young person is homeless or a runaway, that person may have to engage in sex to survive or may be trafficked sexually by others. Of all homeless and runaway youth in the United States, 40 percent of them identify as gay, lesbian, bisexual, or transgender; and the most frequently cited reasons for their homelessness are that they ran away from home or were forced to leave home because of their parents' rejection of their gender identity or sexual orientation (Human Rights Campaign 2017).

Similarly, according to the traditional gender paradigm, women are to be subordinate to men, and, in the context of the AIDS pandemic, subordination increases the likelihood that women will become infected. In fact, marriage is a major risk factor for women. For example, since they are to be subordinate to their husbands, a wife is not able to negotiate the use of safer sex practices at home—even if she knows her husband is having extramarital affairs (Phiri 2003, 8, 13). Correspondingly, to maintain their dominance, men resort to the use of violence against women, and intimate partner violence and other forms of gender-based violence are related to higher HIV rates for women (Be in the Know 2023).

Researchers and activists involved with the pandemic recognize the harm that unequal gender hierarchies cause both gay men and heterosexual women. One of their objectives is to modify that paradigm to reduce gender inequalities and thereby reduce infection rates. In the limited parameters of this discussion, we can see that traditional gender paradigms privilege heterosexual men at the expense of both MSM and heterosexual women, and that these latter groups are at higher risks of HIV infection as a result. Since the HIV ministries Barnes describes, as well as most theologically conservative churches, uphold the traditional gender paradigms, they were not as effective

---

2. See Leviticus 18:22; 20:13. The same hierarchy appears in Romans 1:12-27.

as they might be, at best, and they increased the vulnerability of MSM and heterosexual women to HIV, at worst.

To counter this dynamic, Black churches on both sides of the Atlantic need to discuss the issues of gender, human sexuality, and homosexuality. Without such basic conversations on gender, these two groups—MSM and heterosexual women—will continue to be disproportionately infected. In the next section, we will utilize insights from John Wesley's legacy to explore additional theological statements that make it difficult for effective prevention programs to be implemented.

The Prosperity Gospel, The Bible, and John Wesley

The Prosperity Gospel and its related neo-Pentecostal and charismatic movements have seen global success, and it is easy to understand why. As discussed above, prosperity messages offer benefits by meeting deep human needs; but in the context of the HIV and AIDS pandemic, these messages are also problematic. Here, I contend that these messages—although there may be a biblical basis for them—prevent the implementation of truly effective HIV prevention programs. Furthermore, I will show that there are other biblical texts with messages that would be more helpful, and that these other messages are more consistent with the legacy of John Wesley. Consequently, in the era of AIDS, Methodist churches would be better served by reclaiming their own heritage than resorting to the Prosperity Gospel.

I have personally heard the statements discussed below over the years I have done HIV-related work. However, I do not claim that I have heard them consistently in each of the countries—South Africa, Brazil, and the United States—and I do not claim that the statements have been endorsed officially by the Methodist denominations in these countries. These are statements, though, that have come from practicing Christians, and they represent beliefs that have been influenced by the Prosperity Gospel and conservative evangelical theology.

Statement One: "If you are HIV positive, it is because you have sinned."

Essentially, the Prosperity Gospel offers "the promise of spiritual, physical, and material blessings for those who follow its tenets" (Barnes 2013, 50). On the one hand, such an underlying assumption means that, if a believer succeeds, that person is being blessed for faithfulness. On the other hand, if a believer experiences any misfortune or setback, then it is because he or she has not followed the faith's tenets and therefore sinned in some way. Within this schema, becoming HIV positive is easily explained as the result of sin. Given the identification of the virus with gay men, promiscuous women, and drug users, all of whom are deemed to have violated conservative sexual and behavioral norms, the statement makes sense. After all, since God punishes because of sin, then an HIV-positive person has been simply punished for her or his sin. The impact of such an understanding, though, is to increase stigma and discrimination against persons living with HIV, which limits the willingness of HIV-positive persons to get tested or to receive treatment.

A scriptural verse (or portion thereof) used in this context is Romans 6:23: "The wages of sin is death." Yet, this problematic use of this verse undercuts HIV prevention efforts. If God punishes sinners, then God has punished the HIV-positive person, and if we work to prevent infections, are we not trying to interfere with what would be God's punishment of the person? Such a reading is also harmful for two additional reasons. First, it misinterprets the text. Basic exegetical work connects this verse with a broader discussion in the whole chapter. Paul considers slavery to sin to have been "death," but "sin" here does not refer to specific individual actions. Furthermore, such slavery ends with baptism in Christ, at which point, the believer gains sanctification and eternal life (Kitteridge 2014, 406). The "death" referred to in the verse is figurative and not literal. In contrast, the physical consequences of (untreated) HIV infections could mean a literal and not figurative death.

Second, such a reading misrepresents the full biblical witness. It may comfort Christians to think that the only ones who suffer are those who sin, but that is simply not the case. Bad things do happen to good people, and the Bible acknowledges that fact. Job is a righteous man who suffers but proclaims his innocence, and his friends try to convince him that God is punishing or disciplining him because of sin. In Job 42:7, God expresses anger at Job's friends because they "have not spoken of me what is right, as my servant Job has." After reading the book of Job, we do not know why suffering occurs—but we do know that it is not because those persons have sinned.

Similarly, the New Testament relates an encounter between Jesus and a blind man. The disciples ask Jesus, "Rabbi, who sinned, this man or his parents, that he was born blind?" and Jesus answers, "Neither this man nor his parents sinned; he was born blind so that God's works might be revealed in him" (John 9:2-3). As in the book of Job, the assumed connection between sin and suffering is disrupted. Moreover, Jesus' healing of the blind man reveals God's glory and Jesus' divine sonship (Reinhartz 2014, 285). In the context of the HIV pandemic, these texts in Job and John counter the misuse of Romans 6:23 in the Prosperity Gospel. Instead of condemning those who are HIV positive, we can focus on compassion and healing in the name of Jesus Christ.

How might the works of John Wesley inform this matter? On two important issues, the poor and slavery, Wesley refused to "blame the unfortunate for their own conditions." Concerning the poor, Wesley rejected the typical notion of his day (and our own) that the poor are poor "only because they are idle," as seen in this excerpt from his Journal dated February 9–10, 1753.

> On Friday and Saturday I visited as many more [sick] as I could. I found some in their cells underground, others in their garrets, half starved both with cold and hunger, added to weakness and pain. But I found not one of them unemployed who was able to crawl about the room. So wickedly, devilishly false is the common objection, "They are poor because they are idle" (*Works*, 20:445).

Similarly, in his day, the enslavement of Africans was justified based on, among other things, their supposed inferiority, a proposition that Wesley rejected. According to him, "certainly the African is in no respect inferior to the European." From his theological perspective, all persons were "equally depraved" but also "equally the recipients of God's grace" (Brendlinger 2006, 68). Wesley saw the harm caused by attributing the suffering or misfortune of whole groups of people to their status or deeds (or lack thereof)—and we should as well. Rather than the Romans text and views of the Prosperity Gospel, the message of the books of Job and John is the better one to use in the age of AIDS, and it is the more Methodist one.

Statement Two: "I know that the culture is more affirming of women and gays, but I'm going to hold fast to the Bible."

In many respects, the Prosperity Gospel has been influenced by multiple traditions, and one is evangelicalism and its conservative political impulses. Even though Word of Faith pastors have not emphasized "hot-button issues," they support them based on their reading of Scripture. Word of Faith teachers have successfully reached across political, generational, and racial lines due to their emphases on Scripture, prophecy, healing, and wealth rather than the political issues that have largely defined the American culture wars. This is not to say, however, that the theology of the Word of Faith movement is inconsistent with conservative political currents. Abortion, homosexuality, the teaching of evolution, and any form of religious pluralism are all generally rejected as counter to their interpretation of Scripture (Attanasi and Yong 2012, 119).

A scriptural reading that seems to support the concept of "holding fast" against liberal developments in society is Romans 12:2: "Do not be conformed to this world, but be transformed by the renewing of your minds." The scriptural texts themselves, though, indicate a range of possible interpretations concerning heterosexual women and gay men, the two groups that are disproportionately affected by the HIV pandemic. For example, the normative gender paradigm for male/female relationships is usually a hierarchical one, based on Genesis 3:16, but a more mutual and interdependent one is found in the Song of Songs (Anderson 2016). Similarly, same-sex relationships are condemned, at least in part, because they are non-procreative relationships. Deuteronomy 23:1 forbids the admission to the assembly of anyone "whose testicles are crushed or whose penis is cut off." However, Isaiah 56:3-5 specifically includes eunuchs, and Acts 8:26-40 describes the baptism and inclusion of an Ethiopian eunuch. These biblical contrasts are mentioned here to illustrate the diversity in the biblical witness, and that different interpretations of Scripture on these two topics are possible.

Over time, Methodist denominations have adopted conservative evangelical positions on social issues, including gender, and so conform to the surrounding culture. Yet we would do well to remember that those positions have not always been those of John Wesley or Methodism. For example, Wesley supported women preaching during his lifetime. In fact, women had flourishing ministries, but the British conference passed a resolution in 1803 that prohibited women from preaching. Even with women's evangelistic successes, the first reason listed for the decision was simply that "a vast majority of our people are opposed to it" (Chilcote 1991, 236). I am astonished by the fact that Wesley had only died in 1791, which means that there would have been preachers in that gathering who knew Wesley and knew of his support for women, but the resolution passed. Likewise, Wesley was known for his antislavery work, and just days before his death, he wrote a letter of encouragement to William Wilberforce, the abolitionist (Brendlinger 2009, 42).

In spite of conference restrictions concerning slave ownership, the practice continued among Methodists in the southern areas of the United States, and those Methodists split from the northern church, rather than end slavery. Finally, the restrictive language on homosexuality that existed in The UMC's 2016 *Book of Discipline* was first added only in 1972. Unlike the conservative evangelicals and proponents of the Prosperity Gospel, who might consider themselves "holding fast" against a culture perceived as more liberal, United Methodists in the United States have tended to forsake their own tradition and adopted more conservative policies from the surrounding culture. Therefore, Methodists cannot claim that they never adopt the prevalent values from the surrounding culture. Methodists need to know that Wesley's staunch antislavery position was not based on references to the Bible. Wesley in fact "set aside" the necessity of biblical answers on slavery; instead, "he turned to criteria of justice and mercy, asking if the practices described could be reconciled with them (Stone 2011, 194).

Given the extensive impact of HIV on heterosexual women, especially in sub-Saharan Africa, where nearly two-thirds of all HIV-positive persons live, there are church leaders who want to promote a more egalitarian reading of the Bible that will support the dignity of women—but they either ignore the issue of homosexuality or merely attempt to soften the condemnation (Ammann and Holland 2012; McMickle 2008). Such a strategy, though, will eventually fail to counter the negative impact of the pandemic on women because of the underlying assumptions on which traditional gender hierarchies are based. Specifically, traditional gender paradigms assume that men are to be dominant, and women are to be subordinate. That devalued subordinate role prescribed for women is directly related to the disdain held for any such subordinate role for men. With its inherent devaluing of women and hierarchical privileging of men, the traditional gender paradigm must be challenged. Basically, heterosexual women and gay men are devalued in the same way, and it will be ineffective to try to "treat" women better while continuing to condemn homosexuality. The fates of these groups are intimately connected. To reduce new HIV infections, both women and gay men must be accorded dignity and respect.

Statement 3: "All of this death from AIDS is a sign. It means that Christ is returning soon."

Due to staggering numbers of deaths from AIDS in the pandemic, some Christians have discerned resonances with the Book of Revelation and popular concepts of the "rapture," a time of trial and tribulation, and Christ's return. Revelation 20:1–5 speaks of a thousand-year period (millennium), where evil seems to be bound, but questions remain about the details. As summarized by Wesleyan studies scholar Douglas Strong, a perspective known as premillennialism emphasizes the imminent coming of Christ and the destruction of the world as we know it, "prior to the establishment of the millennial reign of God on earth." Adopted by conservative evangelicals such as Dwight L. Moody (1837–1899), it deems the Christian's task to be evangelism—"saving souls"—and "there is no place for social restructuring because the world is simply getting worse." The postmillennial perspective, in contrast, is exemplified by the Social Gospel movement and Walter Rauschenbusch (1861–1918). It more optimistically views God's plan for the world less "with a cataclysmic millennial consummation of God's rule." Instead, it emphasizes "the present Kingdom of God—a 'realized eschatology.'" From this perspective, social transformation is possible and seems consistent with the Lord's

Prayer in Matthew 6:10: "Your kingdom come . . . Your will be done on earth as it is in heaven" (Strong 1997, xxx–xxxii).

For our purposes, the difference between postmillennial and premillennial theologies is that the former allows consideration of current systemic social and economic struggles, whereas the latter tends not to do so. In general, conservative evangelical and Pentecostal theologies tend to focus on individual behavior rather than the systemic issues affecting that behavior, and both of these traditions influence the Prosperity Gospel. Consequently, the Prosperity Gospel seeks to assist people's "self-actualization" while ignoring "structural inequalities that undermine any attempt at self-actualization" (Day 2012, 110). Yet the myriad systemic factors that shape individual behavior are pivotal in the context of HIV and AIDS (Dube 2008, 173). Thus, "we can only sufficiently deal with HIV and AIDS when we also focus on both individual and structural evils and social injustice issues that affect the individual's choices and decisions" (Dube 2008, 173).

Unlike those who uphold the Prosperity Gospel, John Wesley was a post-millennialist, holding "that the incipient presence of the Reign of God in our world is a growing reality, spurred on by the expectation of a penultimate fulfillment of that Reign prior to the New Creation" (Maddox 1994, 240). Wesley advocated a "truly holistic salvation" that includes wholeness of body and spirit in the present (Maddox 2007, 7). More focused on current reality than the afterlife, Wesley emphasized compassion for the poor as part of the Christian commitment to love one's neighbor (Marquardt 1992, 31). His efforts on behalf of the poor were numerous and included establishing a medical clinic, offering revolving loans (micro-lending), and starting the Kingswood School for poor children (Stone 2001, 102–3).

As mentioned above, Wesley knew that the poor were not poor because they were lazy. Moreover, he identified those groups that tended to benefit from exploiting the poor: merchants, distillers, doctors, and lawyers (Jennings 1990, 72–78). Wesley's critique of wealth gained at the expense of the poor may even form an early expression of "a preferential option for the poor." For our purposes, though, the crucial element is that Wesley "demystified wealth" so that wealth and power are not "the sign of divine favor" and "the models of faith," while poverty is not "seen as an indication of divine disapproval," or "as punishment for sins of sloth or unbelief" (Jennings 1990, 47). Wesley's writings thus offer a critique of the gospel of wealth and success, that is, the Prosperity Gospel. Such a critique reminds us that the Prosperity Gospel is not consistent with Wesley's legacy and encourages us to determine the dynamics that exploit the poor today (Withrow 2007). Since nearly two thirds of all persons living with HIV live in sub-Saharan Africa and are disproportionately poor, following Wesley's lead would help us to address some of the systemic drivers of new HIV infections, rather than see the related deaths as a divine sign.

Methodist Re-Readings of the Bible in the Context of HIV and AIDS

It is worth noting that, for each of the problematic statements discussed in the previous section, biblical passages were cited in support of the statement and others that opposed it. Obviously, both sides can claim that their position is biblically based; the broader question must be whether one perspective more fully reflects the will of God in this time and place.

As a Bible scholar, I know that, since the biblical texts were written by human beings, they are contextual, and we should consider the differences between those contexts and our own when we interpret these biblical texts today. Furthermore, as a Methodist, I believe that these texts were "breathed into" by God (inspired) and that the work of the Holy Spirit in shaping these texts helps communities of faith to interpret them today. I refer to these as Methodist understandings here because they were actually held by John Wesley.

John Wesley, whose commitment to the Bible as Scripture is undisputed, affirmed the importance of the original biblical languages over translations; consulted a variety of English, French, and German translations; read the Bible with the standard scholarly tools of his day; and could acknowledge the role of human authors and therefore the cultural specificity of biblical texts (Maddox 2011). Additionally, he knew that "we need the same spirit to understand the Scripture which enabled the holy men of old to *write* it" (Maddox

2011, 14). Acknowledging the ancient context of biblical texts means that it is the interpretive process itself that gives a text meaning. As Robert Wall writes, "the 'plain sense' of every canonical text unfolds throughout its history as every talented interpreter adapts its meaning to ever-changing social locations" (Wall 1995, 54).

For our purposes, it is most important to consider how Wesley read the Bible. As shown below, he has at least three approaches that can help us identify a Methodist approach. First, Wesley read the biblical canon as a whole, which reflected "his commitment to the theological and spiritual value of the whole Bible" (Maddox 2011, 16). He also assumed that biblical passages should be read comparatively with other passages (Maddox 2012, 8). Applying these insights to the contrasting passages discussed here means that neither passage should be considered "the" determinative meaning on its own, and that both sets of passages need to be evaluated within the theological and spiritual value of the whole Bible.

Second, Wesley emphasized the importance of reading the Bible in conference with other readers, even those who disagreed with him (Maddox 2011, 18–19). The goal of this openness to dialogue with others was to reach "the most adequate understandings," and he "specifically invited any who believed that he presented mistaken readings of the Bible in his Sermons to be in touch, so that they could confer together over Scripture" (Maddox 2011, 19). In the context of the HIV pandemic, it is crucial that Methodists who adhere to traditional paradigms on gender and sexuality confer with those with whom they disagree, including those living with the virus. They need to learn how the Bible is read differently by those who are HIV positive, and to hear from them about the physical and emotional damage caused by those traditional values. Under these circumstances, learning and hearing from persons living with HIV is consistent with Wesley's concept of "global listening," which, in turn, reflects his understanding of the "catholic spirit" (Bryant 2017). To live out that "catholic spirit" by engaging with those often deemed "Other" is compatible with our Methodist heritage.

Determining Christian policies and doctrine without considering the "Other" is especially problematic in the context of HIV and AIDS, because those deemed "Other" are the ones who are disproportionately affected by the pandemic. As a result, those who are most affected by the pandemic are not the ones who set "the" Christian perspectives on handling the pandemic, including the determination of acceptable prevention strategies. We need an interpretive lens to help us develop readings that truly apply to all Christians. Fortunately, John Wesley provides such an interpretive lens.

The most distinctive feature of how Wesley read the Bible is the way he used 1 John 4:19, "We love [God] because he first loved us," as the interpretive lens through which the rest of Scripture should be read (Maddox 2011, 26–27; Wall 2010, 113–28). Randy Maddox notes that Wesley preached on or alluded to 1 John more than any other biblical book; he finds that, after his Aldersgate experience, Wesley came to fully understand that the "enduring love of God and others is a response to knowing God's pardoning love for us" (Maddox 2011, 26–28).

Maddox refers to Wesley's distinctive emphasis on "God's universal pardoning and transforming love," and I wonder if that interpretive lens can help us move away from traditional readings of Scripture that harm many Christians. Considering Wesley's interpretive practices, and nudged by the Spirit, I have "updated" Romans 8:38–39 to show how that universal love could be expressed in the midst of the HIV pandemic.

> For I am convinced that neither death, nor life, nor angels, nor rulers,
> nor things present, nor things to come, nor height, nor depth,
> nor male nor female, nor gay nor straight,
> nor cisgender nor transgender,
> nor being HIV positive or being HIV negative,
> nor being high class, or having no class at all,
> nor powers, nor anything else in all creation,
> will be able to separate us from the love of God
> in Christ Jesus our Lord. (Author Translation)

Clearly, my inclusive and contextual reading of Romans 8:38–39 is different from the biblical one, and it necessarily raises the issue of biblical authority. Biblical authority is usually thought of in hierarchical terms; traditional readings are thought to come "from above," and our task as persons of faith is to submit to them. Another option is to redefine "biblical authority," and several scholars in the Wesleyan tradition have reconceptualized it as a relational dynamic, rather than a hierarchical one. For example, Wall argues that Wesley did not think Scripture's authority was "unilateral and absolute," but that it was instead "conversational and relational" (Wall 1995, 59; Lancaster 2001, 198).

Similarly, our notion of inspiration must be reconceptualized. When we think of the Bible as "inspired" by God, traditionally we think of it "being a 'deposit' of true information dropped down coercively on scribes who simply penned the work" (Stone 1995, 126). Instead, Bryan Stone proposes that it is a type of dialogue that offers us the possibility of "a healed humanity."

> "Inspiration" refers to the transforming power of grace that does not negate human frailty, error, and other limitations with which we all live as human beings (for example, the patriarchy of the biblical witnesses), but rather enters into "dialogue" with our wounded and limited humanity and poses to it the possibility of a healed humanity.

In this view, biblical authority is an educational process, and we look to the Bible "for how the biblical witnesses 'learned how to learn' from within their own context, experience, and understanding. What we are ultimately looking for is the movement, trajectory, and dynamics of an educational process leading us toward the fullest expression of the *imago dei* in our lives" (Stone 1995, 129). Stone's concept of biblical authority as "divine pedagogy" means that we remain open to challenges to our own experiences and understandings as we engage the biblical text (Stone 1995, 131).

Basically then, a Methodist rereading of the Bible is one that reminds us of God's universal love that is open to all (1 John) and engages us in an educational process where the goal is for us to become a new community of healed humanity. Unlike the Prosperity Gospel, with its fixed interpretations concerning gender and sexuality, the Methodist tradition offers the possibility of biblical rereadings. We can use God's universal love as an interpretive lens that allows us to affirm the *imago Dei* within ourselves and others and move us toward full inclusion for all. In the context of HIV and AIDS, that message offered by Methodist denominations would be good news indeed!

Conclusion

Without a doubt, the Prosperity Gospel is popular globally. As a result, Methodist denominations in South Africa, Brazil, and the United States have incorporated some of its theological tenets. However, the Methodist tradition itself can offer many of the same advantages that the Prosperity Gospel offers, without its negative consequences. For example, the Prosperity Gospel offers a renewed self-esteem and sense of hope—especially to those who have often been socially and economically marginalized. One of the roots of that theological affirmation is Arminianism, which supports the possibility of universal salvation for all and opposes theories of limited atonement. Such a theological stance, though, is not unique to the Prosperity Gospel or the Pentecostal tradition from which it comes. To the contrary, both Methodists and Pentecostals have that Arminian tradition, and it would be good for Methodists to reaffirm it.

Similarly, the Prosperity Gospel is applauded for the upward social mobility achieved by some of its followers, but that same dynamic happened with early Methodists, even during Wesley's lifetime (Tomkins 2003; Everts 215). Yet Wesley had a maxim by which he himself lived: "Earn all you can; save all you can; give all you can." Apparently, his followers took the third part of the maxim, "Give all you can," less literally than did Wesley himself (Tomkins 2003, 184). Nevertheless, the maxim is part of Methodist heritage and can be reclaimed to emphasize that the accumulation of wealth is not in and of itself the goal of the Christian life, as it is thought to be, to a large extent, in the Prosperity Gospel.

Finally, the health aspect of the "Health and Wealth" gospel also has a precedent from Wesley's era. Wesley established a free medical clinic in London in the 1740s, and, about that time, his collection of home remedies, *Primitive Physick*, was published for the first time. That volume "went through 23 editions in Wesley's lifetime . . . and stayed in print (and use!) until the 1880s" (Maddox 2007, 4). Plus, Wesley's lay assistants were to know its contents and have the book with them when they made pastoral visits (Maddox 2007, 8–9). For our purposes here, a significant feature of Wesley's commitments to health and healing is that he "did not reject professional medical care, in favor of sole reliance on either traditional treatments or divine healing." Instead, Wesley affirmed both divine and medical healing (Maddox 2007, 10–11). This aspect of his legacy on health contrasts sharply with the message, given in some Prosperity Gospel circles, that HIV can be cured by divine healing alone. Returning to Wesley's understanding could be an important corrective for Methodist denominations.

For the final word, we will return to 1 John, the biblical text that John Wesley so favored. First John is one of three Johannine letters. They were written to churches that were "struggling with false teaching and false prophets," and the author "writes to encourage his readers to continue embracing and putting into play in their lives the truth that they had received—and, in so doing, to ward off the influence of false teachers" (Green 2010, 141). In the context of HIV and AIDS, this message still rings true: Methodist denominations should embrace and put into play what we have received from John Wesley, and so ward off negative influences of the Prosperity Gospel.

References

Ammann, Arthur J. with Julie Ponsford Holland. 2012. *Women, HIV, and the Church: In Search of Refuge.* Eugene, OR: Cascade Books.

Anderson, Cheryl B. "Negotiating the Prosperity Gospel and Methodist Denominational Identity in the Age of Aids." In *Wesleyan Communities and the World Beyond Christianity*, edited by Ted A. Campbell, 125–58. Nashville: Wesley's Foundery Books.

———. 2016. "Song of Songs: Redeeming Gender Constructions in the Age of AIDS." In *Womanist Interpretations of the Bible: Expanding the Discourse*, edited by Gay L. Byron and Vanessa Lovelace, 73–92. Atlanta: SBL Press.

Attanasi, Katherine and Amos Yong. 2012. *Pentecostalism and Prosperity: The Socio-Economics of the Global Charismatic Movement.* New York: Palgrave Macmillan.

Barnes, Sandra. 2013. *Live Long and Prosper: How Black Megachurches Address HIV/AIDS and Poverty in the Age of Prosperity Theology.* New York: Fordham University Press.

Be in The Know. 2023 "Gender Inequality and HIV." Updated March 30, 2023. https://www.beintheknow.org/understanding-hiv-epidemic/context/gender-inequality-and-hiv.

Brendlinger, Irv A. 2006. *Social Justice through the Eyes of John Wesley: John Wesley's Theological Challenge to Slavery*. Ontario, Canada: Joshua Press.

Brown Douglas, Kelly. 1999. *Sexuality and the Black Church: A Womanist Perspective*. Maryknoll, NY: Orbis Books.

Bryant, Barry. 2017. "Contextual and Connectional: 'Hearing' the Scripture." May 16, 2017. http://www.umglobal.org/2017/05/barry-bryant-contextual-connectional.html.

Chilcote, Paul. 1991. *John Wesley and the Women Preachers of Early Methodism*. Metuchen, NJ: Scarecrow Press.

Cohen, Cathy J. 1999. *Boundaries of Blackness: AIDS and the Breakdown of Black Politics*. Chicago: University of Chicago Press.

Day, Keri. 2012. *Unfinished Business: Black Women, the Black Church, and the Struggle to Thrive in America*. Maryknoll, NY: Orbis Books.

Dube, Musa Wenkosi. 2008. *The HIV and AIDS Bible: Selected Essays*. Scranton, PA: University of Scranton Press.

Everts, Janet Meyer. 2015. "Living to Give: The Prosperity Gospel in Global Context and Biblical Perspective." Unpublished paper presented at the International Society of Biblical Literature Meeting in Buenos Aires, Argentina. July 21, 2015.

Fewell, Danna Nolan and David M. Gunn. 1993. *Gender, Power & Promise: The Subject of the Bible's First Story*. Nashville: Abingdon Press.

Furre, Berge. 2006. "Crossing Boundaries: The 'Universal Church' and the Spirit of Globalization." In *Spirits of Globalization: The Growth of Pentecostalism and Experiential Spiritualities in a Global Age*, edited by Sturla Stalsett, 48–49. London: SCM Press.

Green, Joel B. 2010. *Reading Scripture as Wesleyans*. Nashville: Abingdon Press.

Harris, Angelique. 2010. *AIDS, Sexuality, and the Black Church: Making the Wounded Whole*. New York: Peter Lang.

Human Rights Campaign. 2017. "New Report on Youth Homeless Affirms that LGBTQ Youth Disproportionately Experience Homelessness." November 15, 2017. https://www.hrc.org/news/new-report-on-youth-homeless-affirms-that-lgbtq-youth-disproportionately-ex.

Jennings Jr., Theodore W. 1990. *Good News for the Poor: John Wesley's Evangelical Economics*. Nashville: Abingdon Press.

Kitteridge, Cynthia Briggs. 2014. "Romans." In *Fortress Commentary on the Bible: The New Testament*, edited by Margaret Aymer, Cynthia Briggs Kitteridge, and David A. Sanchez, x, 395–426. Minneapolis: Fortress Press.

Lancaster, Sarah Heaner. 2001. "What Does the Authority of the Bible Mean for United Methodists?" *Quarterly Review* 21 no. 2 (Summer): 194–200.

Maddox, Randy L. 1994. *Responsible Grace: John Wesley's Practical Theology.* Nashville: Kingswood Books.

———. 2007. "John Wesley on Holistic Health and Healing," *Methodist History* 46, no. 1: 4–33.

———. 2011. "The Rule of Christian Faith, Practice, and Hope: John Wesley on the Bible," *Methodist Review* 3: 2–12.

———. 2012. "John Wesley—A Man of One Book." In *Wesley, Wesleyans, and Reading the Bible as Scripture*, edited by Joel B. Green and David F. Watson, 3–18. Waco: Baylor University Press.

Marquardt, Manfred. 1992. *John Wesley's Social Ethics: Praxis and Principles.* Translated by John F. Seely and W. Stephen Gunter. Nashville: Abingdon Press.

Martin, Dale B. 2006. *Sex and the Single Savior: Gender and Sexuality in Biblical Interpretation.* Louisville: Westminster John Knox Press.

McGee, Paula L. 2017. *Brand® New Theology: the Wal-Martization of T. D. Jakes and the New Black Church.* Maryknoll, NY: Orbis Books.

McMickle, Marvin A. 2008. *A Time to Speak: How Black Pastors Can Respond to the HIV/AIDS Pandemic.* Cleveland: Pilgrim Press.

Miller, Donald E. and Tetsunao Yamamori, *Global Pentecostalism: The New Face of Christian Social Engagement.* Berkeley, CA: University of California Press, 2007.

Mitchem, Stephanie Y. 2007. *Name It and Claim It? Prosperity Preaching in the Black Church.* Cleveland: Pilgrim Press.

Phiri, Isabel Apawo. 2003. "African Women of Faith Speak Out in an HIV/AIDS Era." In *African Women, HIV/AIDS and Faith Communities*, eds. Isabel Apawo Phiri, Beverley Haddad, and Madipoane Masenya (ngwana' Mphahlele), 3–20. Pietermaritzburg, South Africa: Cluster Books.

Reinhartz, Adele. 2014. "John." In *Fortress Commentary on the Bible: The New Testament*, edited by Margaret Aymer, Cynthia Briggs Kitteridge, and David A. Sánchez, 265–307. Minneapolis: Fortress Press.

Stone, Bryan P. 2005. "Wesleyan Theology, Scriptural Authority, and Homosexuality." *Wesley Theological Journal* 30 no. 2 (Fall): 108–38.

Stone, Ronald H. 2001. *John Wesley's Life and Ethics.* Nashville: Abingdon Press.

Strong, Douglas M. 1997. *They Walked in the Spirit: Personal Faith and Social Action in America.* Louisville: Westminster John Knox Press.

Tomkins, Stephen. 2003. *John Wesley: A Biography*. Grand Rapids: Eerdmans.

Wall, Robert W. 1995. "Toward a Wesleyan Hermeneutics of Scripture," *Wesleyan Theological Journal* 10, no. 2: 50–67.

———. 2010. "Wesley as Biblical Interpreter." In *The Cambridge Companion to John Wesley*, edited by Randy L. Maddox and Jason E. Vickers, 113–28. New York: Cambridge University Press.

Walton, Jonathan L. 2014. "Prosperity Gospel and African American Theology." In *The Oxford Handbook of African American Theology*, edited by Anthony B. Pinn and Katie G. Cannon, 453–467. New York: Oxford University Press.

Wesley, John. 1991. *Journal and Diaries III (1745–1754)*. Edited by W. Reginald Ward and Richard P. Heitzenrater. Vol. 20 of the *Bicentennial Edition of the Works of John Wesley*. Nashville, Abingdon Press.

Withrow, Lisa R. 2007. "Success and the Prosperity Gospel: From Commodification to Transformation—A Wesleyan Perspective," *Journal of Religious Leadership* 6, no. 2:15–41.

CHAPTER 3

Wesley's Ecologically Informed Interpretation of Scripture, Science, and Society[1]

Presian R. Burroughs

Like Wesley before us, we face moral, practical, and socio-political crises. One such crisis touches the entire human population: the diminishing health and vitality of God's creation. When we consider global as well as local environmental and social concerns—e.g., global warming and food insecurity—we encounter heated debates about how to respond in economical, practicable, equitable, and sustainable ways. If we, as Wesleyan Christians, are to approach such debates with Wesleyan-inspired wisdom, we need to interpret both Scripture and society carefully. Thankfully, we have an exemplar for this endeavor in John Wesley himself, for he drew upon the best theological, scientific, and sociological resources of his day to teach his communities and confront those in power. As a result, he unconsciously modeled an ecologically informed interpretation of Scripture, science, and society that we too can implement today.

---

1. This essay is adapted from a previous publication, Burroughs 2021.

We may be surprised to learn that John Wesley stands out as a remarkably creation-attuned Christian leader of the early modern era. As expressed in "The General Deliverance" (Sermon 60), he believed in the future restoration, and even glorification, of nonhuman creatures. This sets him apart from many who would consider God's work of salvation to extend only to humanity. "The General Deliverance" can, therefore, function as a necessary corrective to narrower theologies and inspire us with hope and vision during our current ecological crisis. However, if we consult this sermon without attention to Wesley's other writings, we may get the impression that he held a rather negative view of nonhuman creatures in their present condition. This is because Wesley here portrayed animals as fierce, cruel, and deformed in this time between Adam and Eve's transgression and the arrival of the new creation. That perspective does not, however, capture Wesley's fullest portrait of the natural world.

Wesley's often-neglected work, *A Survey of the Wisdom of God in the Creation: A Compendium of Natural Philosophy* (1810 edition title), provides a thoroughgoing and appreciative interpretation of creation. It also offers a helpful counterbalance to the unfavorable depiction of animals we encounter in "The General Deliverance." The *Compendium* is a five-part work first published in 1763. It presents the natural world as revelatory of the Creator God and as displaying balance, harmony, complexity, wisdom, interdependence, and even tenderness. In this expansive work, Wesley compiled, interpreted, and translated some of his era's best science (understood then as "natural philosophy"). Although the *Compendium* educates individuals and families on the workings of creation and even sometimes inspires them to adore creation and worship the Creator, it does not specifically address how human societies exploit and inequitably distribute God's blessings (what we often call "natural resources"). The *Compendium* consequently may lead readers to assume that observing and appreciating creation is an individualistic and, perhaps, even an amoral endeavor—one that is to be performed without corporate calls to action.

Yet, when we include a third sample from Wesley's corpus into our mix, we find that Wesley believed principled Christian leaders could influence entire societies and social systems to live in greater harmony with nonhuman creation and with each other. In "Thoughts on the Present Scarcity of Provisions" ([1773] 1996), Wesley illustrated some of the ways Britain's economy was unjust and unhealthy. He argued it should instead promote healthier, more equitable, and more sustainable relationships among people, as well as between people and nature. Wesley's concern for the relationships between and among humans, animals, and land displays the beginnings of an ecological sensibility. Although the field of ecology had not yet developed, it would come to focus on *relationships* between and among living things and nonliving things. By advocating for more efficient and nourishing uses of grains, greater access to arable land among Britain's common people, and less luxury and waste, Wesley displayed an ecologically inspired approach to societal problems. He thereby called his society to embody greater ecological health and well-being.

Each of these three works offers a slightly different perspective on creation, as well as human and divine relationships with the nonhuman creation. We will, therefore, consider them in turn. First, we will consult "The General Deliverance" to consider Wesley's ecological approach to interpreting Scripture and the way of salvation, including his bold conclusion that God will liberate and provide recompense for nonhuman creatures. Second, we will highlight a few portions of Wesley's *Compendium* to discover his ecological interpretation of science and his attention to creation's interdependence and balance as well as its revelatory nature. Third, we will probe his ecological interpretation of society as we reflect on his analysis of Britain's food system in "Thoughts on the Present Scarcity of Provisions." With these three facets of his thought in view, we will close with several interpretive principles and practices that inform a Wesleyan ecological interpretive framework.

Wesley's Ecological Interpretation of Scripture

In his sermon titled "The General Deliverance" (Sermon 60), Wesley modeled an ecological approach to interpreting Romans 8:19-22. In this section of Romans, Paul discusses creation's eager anticipation of humanity's impending resurrection, creation's present and past slavery to destruction, and creation's future liberation into the glory of God's children (Burroughs 2022). Paul does this to help followers of Christ remain confident in God's work of salvation even amid persecution (8:19, 21, 22, 24, 35). By referring to creation in this way, Paul gives us some poignant and instructive statements on God's intentions for the nonhuman creation. Many interpreters misconstrue or ignore these statements, but Wesley grappled carefully with the nonhuman aspects of Romans 8:19-22.

Wesley's Attention to Nonhuman Creation in Scripture

As in Romans, Wesley's sermon, "The General Deliverance," includes reflections on the nonhuman creation itself and does not focus solely on divine relationships. This may not appear terribly momentous since Romans 8:19-22 explicitly refers to "creation" or "creature." However, since the early centuries of the church, prominent Christian leaders had understood the word "creature" (KJV) or "creation" (NRSV, NIV) in Romans 8:19-22 to refer to *human* creatures. But John Wesley more accurately recognized that it refers to nonhuman members of creation (Burroughs 2022). In other words, Wesley had the interpretive sensibility to perceive with Paul that God intends to liberate nonhuman creatures along with human beings.

Wesley set the stage for this conclusion by highlighting several passages in Scripture that illustrate God's loving care for all creatures. He reminded his audience that the Creator God "sendeth the springs into the rivers, that run among the hills, to give drink to every beast of the field" (Wesley 1999, 0.1; cf., Ps. 104:10-11). God's kindness towards all creation illustrated a particular moral lesson to Wesley, namely that people should "be tender of even the meaner [lower] creatures; to show mercy to these also" (Wesley 1999, 0.1) Theologically, God's kindness indicated to Wesley that God's work of saving and perfecting would include not only humanity but also the whole gamut of creation. Wesley understood Paul to express precisely this claim in Romans 8:19-22.

Wesley's Attention to Relationships and Cause and Effect

With God's care for creation clearly in view, Wesley offered an additional claim: although God had created all things perfectly good and harmonious—without suffering, violence, or death (Wesley 1999, I.1–2)—the first humans' transgression introduced these negative experiences into people's lives (see Gen. 3; Rom. 5:12-21). But Wesley believed that these consequences also applied to animals. Nonhuman creatures shifted from perfect harmony into a "season of vanity" since, according to Romans 8:20, "the creature was made subject to vanity" (KJV; Wesley 1999, II.6). Beyond the suffering and violence animals experience from each other, Wesley also emphasized that they "are exposed to the violence and cruelty of him that is now their common enemy—man" (Wesley 1999, II.6). Paul did not unpack what this vanity entailed or what the "bondage to corruption" (8:21 KJV) meant for creation. Yet Wesley perceived that these conditions resulted, at least in part, from human action. He not only believed human sin initiated these problems in creation but also perpetuated them. According to Wesley, human cruelty, violence, and even greed caused and continue to cause tremendous amounts of suffering among God's valued, nonhuman creatures (Wesley 1999, II.6; Wesley 1996, I.6).

Wesley took his theology of creation a step further than Paul. Wesley claimed that not only did the first human transgression lead into a world of violence and suffering, but it also prevented God's blessings from continuing to flow to the nonhuman creation. This was because, according to Wesley, God had made human beings to be "viceregents" over creation and had established humanity as a conduit for God's blessings to flow to the rest of creation (Wesley 1999, I.3). Wesley argued, "As all the blessings of God in paradise flowed through man to the inferior creatures; as man was the great channel of communication, between the Creator and the whole brute creation; so when man made himself incapable of transmitting those blessings, that communication was necessarily cut off" (Wesley 1999, II.1). In other words, sin interrupted the movement of blessings between God and nonhuman creatures. As a result, animals experienced vanity on a continual basis (Rom. 8:20 KJV).

Beyond this loss of blessing, Wesley believed Adam and Eve's sin caused animals to live in "savage fierceness" and "unrelenting cruelty;" to have "deformed" and "grisly" appearances; and to "preserve their own lives . . . by destroying their fellow-creatures" (Wesley 1999, II.3–4). All of these characteristics contrast sharply with how God had created nonhuman creatures in the first place and how God ultimately would transform them for the new creation, as Wesley explained later in his sermon (Wesley 1999, III. 4, 6).

Wesley's Attention to God's Redemptive Future

Although human sin and cruelty had marred and harmed creation, Wesley trusted that God had not merely consigned people to violent and cruel behaviors in this age. As a voice-piece of God, he invited people to restrain their selfish passions and instead live according to God's design for human society *and* the rest of creation. Human relationships with God's nonhuman creatures, according to Wesley, should reflect how those relationships will be in the new creation, in the future liberation God has in store for animals. Echoing Romans 8:21, Wesley encouraged his listeners to "look forward beyond this present scene of bondage, to the happy time when [animals] will be delivered therefore into the liberty of the children of God" (Wesley 1999, III.10).

Especially surprising is that Wesley did not think new creatures would simply be created for the new creation but that previously living and suffering animals would be restored to life. We can infer this from Wesley's explanation that creatures' "groans are not dispersed in idle air, but enter into the ears of Him that made them" (Wesley 1999, III.1). God is not ignorant of their plight but will provide a "recompence [*sic*] for what they once suffered" so that "they shall enjoy happiness suited to their state, without alloy, without interruption, and without end" (Wesley 1999, III.4). In short, the animals that had suffered cruelty and violence will receive amends in the eschaton.

Consequently, Wesley argued that animals will experience a form of resurrection and glorification along with human beings.

> The whole brute creation will then, undoubtedly, be restored, not only to the vigour, strength, and swiftness which they had at their creation, but to a

far higher degree of each than they ever enjoyed. They will be restored, not only to that measure of understanding which they had in paradise, but to a degree of it as much higher than that, as the understanding of an elephant is beyond that of a worm (Wesley 1999, III.3).

According to Wesley, this eschatological vision—especially as it emphasized God's care and attentiveness to all creatures—functions to "soften our hearts" and "enlarge our hearts towards those poor creatures" even now, before we fully enter God's liberation in the new creation (Wesley 1999, III.10). In other words, God's future deliverance of nonhuman creation and God's present compassionate care for it ought to motivate Christians to relieve creatures from their present vain sufferings.

Wesley's Interpretation of Scripture and Our Context

How might we appropriate a Wesley-inspired interpretation of Romans 8:19-22? Three notable themes rise to the surface. First is a Wesleyan appreciation of biblical texts that give attention to nonhuman members of creation. Second is a serious recognition that human actions can negatively affect creation and its creatures. Third, by implication, a Wesleyan perspective suggests that people have a theological and moral responsibility to treat God's creatures with kindness and respect and also to reduce their suffering as much as possible. This third theme rests on the confident hope that God is at work rectifying the injustices, violence, and suffering in creation and moving it towards liberation and even glorification.

Even as we allow these hermeneutical and theological perspectives to shape our interpretations of Scripture and creation, we may simultaneously question and ultimately reject some of Wesley's conclusions. For example, we might question his understanding of human beings as "viceregents." This role, according to "The General Deliverance," establishes humans as conduits for God's blessings upon creation, particularly nonhuman creatures. While we may agree that God may choose to funnel blessings to the natural world through people, we will likely reject Wesley's claim here that God's communication with creation was "cut off" because of human sin (Wesley 1999, II.1).

This claim stands as a rather extreme conclusion since the Scriptures Wesley quotes at the beginning of the sermon undermine it. As Wesley himself noted, God daily provides the blessings of life and nourishment *directly* to all creation. Consequently, people do not dam the flow of all divine blessings from God to the rest of creation. Rather, God's relationship with the whole of creation continues despite human sin. We may therefore temper Wesley's thought and instead conclude that God's provision of blessings—those natural conditions that support vitality and liberty throughout nonhuman creation—are occasionally interrupted or even degraded because of human sin. Thus, while we may consider human sin to be detrimental to the rest of creation, we may still determine that God maintains a positive relationship with the nonhuman creation in spite of human interference and sin.

We might also critique Wesley's highly negative portrait of nonhuman creatures. From this sermon alone, we might reasonably conclude that Wesley saw nothing of beauty, understanding, and kindness in the animal world. Our own relationships with animals may lead us to soften Wesley's one-sided depiction of animals as fierce and cruel even as we know fierceness and cruelty exist in the animal world. Yet beyond our own experience and reason, Wesley's broader corpus gives evidence for a much more positive view of nature. As we will consider more fully below, Wesley's *Compendium of Natural Philosophy* repeatedly glories in the beauty, wisdom, and even parental care displayed among insects, birds, fish, and other animals. In fact, he claimed that creatures' "[n]atural instinct . . . is indeed nothing else than the direction of an All-Wise and All-Powerful mind," and he asked,

> What else teaches birds to build their nests hard or soft, according to the constitution of their young? What else makes them keep so constantly in their nest, during the time of incubation, as if they knew the efficacy of their own warmth, and its aptness for animation? . . . can we behold the spider's net, the silk worm's web, the bees' cells, or the ants' granaries, without being forced to acknowledge the Infinite Wisdom, which directs their unerring steps, and has made them fit to be an emblem of art, industry, and frugality to mankind? (Wesley 1810, V.3.10).

It may seem impossible that the same person could write this description of God's creatures as well as the one found in "The General Deliverance."

Giving Wesley the benefit of the doubt, we may concede that his purpose in writing "The General Deliverance" led him to overemphasize the negative condition of creatures in the present time. That sermon's trajectory suggests that he wanted to stress to his audience how far the world had fallen on account of human sin and how great its need is for God's miraculous salvation. Although Wesley's main point stands—that creatures need God's eschatological liberation and reparation for injustices experienced, especially since human action can negatively affect the rest of creation—his exaggeration of creatures' supposedly horrid state opens the possibility that his audience could form an overly negative and disrespectful view of animals. In such a case, pity, rather than divine care and blessings for animals, would motivate people to act in kindness towards them. I would suggest it is prudent for us today to find more nuanced ways to persuade people that creation is not what the Scriptures indicate it should be and inspire them to treat animals kindly.

Wesley's Ecological Interpretation of Science

"The General Deliverance" paints a rather dismal image of creatures in this age, but Wesley's *Compendium of Natural Philosophy* provides a very different impression. Astoundingly, although Wesley was incredibly busy preaching and leading a revival movement, he invested the time and energy to develop for English readers an accessible and detailed explanation of the most up-to-date scientific interpretations of the natural world. He summarized and even translated Latin explanations of human physiology, zoology, botany, geology, astronomy, and meteorology to enrich his contemporaries with the latest science.

Why would Wesley expend so much effort on these scientific works when he had more "theological" matters to address? In short, Wesley considered the natural world itself to be theologically rich. He believed the natural world reveals God's glory, power, wisdom, generosity, eternity, and otherness. The creation . . .

> picture[s] out the Divine perfections. The firmament every where expanded, with all its starry host, declares the immensity and magnificence, the

power and wisdom of its Creator. Thunder, lightning, storms, earthquakes and volcanos, shew the terror of his wrath. Seasonable rains, sunshine and harvest, denote his bounty and goodness, and demonstrate how he opens his hand, and fills all living things with plenteousness. The constantly succeeding generations of plants and animals, imply the eternity of their first cause. Life subsisting in millions of different forms, shews the vast diffusion of this animating power, and death the infinite disproportion between him and every living thing. (Wesley 1810, II.6.9).

Such awe-inspiring prose articulates a theology in which the nonhuman creation is one means by which people experience and come to know and praise their Creator God. Wesley held this high view of creation even as he recognized our dependence on Scripture for more fully revealing God and the way of salvation.

Wesley not only appreciated nature as revelatory, but he also valued the study of the natural world. He believed that its complexity, diversity, harmony, and interdependence teach people how to value the lives on which they depend. Careful examination of the world shows that God prudently covered it with diverse plants to form the foundation of the food system (Wesley 1770, III.2.7). This teaches us the fundamental importance of plant diversity and abundance. Moreover, grasses can teach us humility since they grow profusely apart from people's work and yet nourish so many creatures (Wesley 1770, IV.3.6). Because of God's design and our utter dependence on creation, Wesley insisted that people should "take notice of, and admire" the plants and other, apparently "insignificant" creatures that God has so carefully and generously provided (Wesley 1770, III.2.7). Doing so will show people that in each region and climate of the world, plants provide enough food for the ecosystems' plant-eating inhabitants, just as God intended, unless, that is, human-wrought forces push ecosystems out of balance.

When things work according to God's design, the natural world always moves toward balance, according to Wesley. Throughout the *Compendium*'s five parts, Wesley repeatedly explained that living things depend on one another and on the nonliving creation for their life and health. Consequently, human and animal lifespans, sizes, and even fertility and mortality rates are constrained by their environments and their relationships with other living things (Wesley 1770, I.1.54.3; I.3.9; II.6.7). Wesley perceived "the balance of creatures" as a manifestation of God's wisdom:

> The whole surface of the terraqueous globe, can afford room and support, to no more than a determinate number of all sorts of creatures. And if they should increase to double or treble the number, they must starve or devour one another. To keep the balance even, the great Author of nature has determined the life of all creatures to such a length, and their increase to such a number, proportioned to their use in the world (Wesley 1770, II.6.7).

This notion of balance is similar to what ecologists now call an ecosystem's carrying capacity. When too many consumers (including humans) overtake an area, imbalance (i.e., suffering, starvation, migration, and death) ensues. We may now question Wesley's precise depiction of global balance, but his recognition of natural ecosystem and biosphere limits remains true.

Even as Wesley confidently presented scientific findings, he recognized the need for humility to guide his ongoing research. He affirmed that people should try to understand God's designs in creation, but he also recognized our limited capacity to do so. He believed that after Adam and Eve's transgression, people could not understand the natural world accurately or completely (Wesley 1810, I.4.3). Despite these limits, Wesley expected people to employ their God-given faculties to observe and comprehend the natural world as much as possible, and to do so with humility and caution. Thus, a truly Wesleyan interpretation of the natural world will be persistent, humble, and teachable. It will even lead the interpreter to admire the creation and its Creator (Wesley 1770, III.2.7).

Yet, although Wesley encouraged people to admire and learn from creation, he also recognized that people can negatively alter environments. Prior to the development of bulldozers and chainsaws, Wesley understood that people could decimate a forest and transform it into a bog. Describing an English bog where Roman coins and ancient trees had been uncovered, Wesley explained that, over a thousand years before, the Romans had cut down a vast span of forest in pursuit of the Britons. This process dammed up a river, which caused flooding of the lowland area. This, in turn, "gave rise to the moors, that increased continually, by earthy matter washed down, the consumption of rotting branches and leaves, and the growth of water-moss, which wonderfully flourishes on rotten grounds" (Wesley 1810, IV.1.16). Although that area had once been farmed, Roman actions had so altered the landscape that traditional cultivation became nearly impossible. This example shows that Wesley—at the cusp of the First Industrial Revolution—was able to perceive the human capacity to change entire ecosystems. Since then, human technologies and powers have only grown, empowering us to alter our environments in ways Wesley never could have imagined.

Throughout his *Compendium*, Wesley exercised an astonishing amount of scientific interest and insight, especially for a busy theologian and church leader. Although some of Wesley's views on nature do not agree with contemporary science, his overall approach to learning from God's creation provides a model for Christian leaders today. We, as Wesleyans, have inherited a tradition that humbly attends to and learns from the created order so that we might better know and glorify our creating God.

Wesley's Ecological Interpretation of Society

With Wesley's views on creation and his creation-wide salvation in place, we can consider how he developed an ecologically attuned social ethic. In his presentation entitled "Thoughts on the Present Scarcity of Provisions," Wesley addressed a topic that many of today's pastors would consider "beyond their pay grade," "too political," or simply of little concern: he humbly, though boldly, addressed inequities in the food system. With ecological consciousness, he highlighted systemic factors that diminished access to food and caused food prices to be prohibitively high for many of Britain's residents. Although he was not an expert on economics, Wesley courageously analyzed and criticized oppressive economic practices. Thus, in addition to demonstrating humility and keen observation, Wesley also exercised courage when he interpreted his world.

During his extensive travels in Britain, Wesley encountered disturbing numbers of people who were impoverished and hungry. It appeared that there was not enough food to feed the populace. In contrast to his contemporaries, who noted only a few reasons for this apparent lack of food, Wesley recognized that the problem was more complex and multifaceted. He pinpointed nine reasons for the excessive hunger and limited access to food plaguing Britain's commoners: unemployment; decline in sales of manufactured goods (and thus fewer employment opportunities); extensive amounts of wheat used to make alcohol rather than food; significant quantities of oats used to feed the increasing number of horses that drew more and more luxury chaises and coaches; fewer cows and lambs being raised and slaughtered because landowners instead chose to raise horses for luxury use and sale; less pork, poultry, and fewer eggs available because small-scale farmers no longer had access to farmland; extensive amounts of food being wasted, especially in the homes of the wealthy; exorbitant land rental prices; and high taxes on account of Britain's large national debt (Wesley 1996, I.1–9). Some of these problems may seem worlds and ages away, while others hit uncomfortably close to home. Either way, Wesley's holistic diagnosis of the causes behind hunger not only reveals his values but also his willingness to express harsh truths to those in power.

Underlying Wesley's critical interpretation of society was his assumption that people should be able to grow their own food on common land or else be able to afford food because they were adequately employed and compensated. Based on his belief that God generously and attentively provides nourishment for all creatures—as expressed in "The General Deliverance" and the *Compendium*—Wesley's theology implies that all people should have access to affordable food. When this was not the case, he believed that something must be done so all could eat. As a preacher and Christian leader, Wesley used his voice and influence to promote the positive social transformations needed to make this a reality.

Wesley wrote his social critique in a time when many people could not afford grain for bread, in part, because so much grain was sold to distilleries. Manufacturers and the government (by way of taxes) reaped significant financial benefits from the production and sale of alcoholic beverages. Nevertheless, Wesley boldly criticized this lucrative sector of the grain economy. As he explained, the distilling industry placed heavy demands on grain production and diverted grains away from their more wholesome use in breads and other foods. Consequently, Wesley was indignant that alcohol production interfered with people's easy access to nutrition. He thus criticized the alcohol industry for making products that not only destroyed the drinker's health but also decreased affordable access to food (Wesley 1996, I.3; II.3).

Because he considered feeding oneself and one's family to be so fundamental, Wesley viewed access to crop and pastureland crucial for the well-being of Britain's common people. But this became increasingly difficult in his day. For centuries, families that did not own land would share and manage public land collectively, so that they all could graze their livestock and raise their crops. However, beginning in the 1300s, people with leadership roles and wealth sometimes lobbied for transitioning common lands into privately owned and controlled estates. England's ensuing peasant revolts—in 1381, 1450, 1549, and 1604–1607—were motivated, in part, by these "enclosures" of public lands (Fairlie 2009, 18). Yet, during Wesley's lifetime, even more strategic and far-reaching enclosure efforts were underway. In fact, "[b]etween 1760 and 1870, about 7 million acres (about one sixth the area of England) were changed, by some 4,000 acts of parliament, from common land to enclosed land" (Fairlie 2009, 25). By bringing common land under private control, Britain's wealthy leaders hoped to "increase efficiency and production" of food, move commoners from country farm work to urban factory work, and then feed the increasing numbers of city dwellers with goods from private estates (Fairlie 2009, 24). These changes proved effective for this agenda. Yet, they forced thousands of common people into poverty and malnutrition because they no longer had the ability to feed themselves through their own agricultural efforts.

Wesley harshly criticized these land reforms. He noted that pork, poultry, and eggs were prohibitively expensive "[b]ecause of the monopolizing of farms," which he considered "as mischievous a monopoly as was ever introduced into these kingdoms." He explained:

> The land which was some years ago divided between ten or twenty little farmers, and enabled them comfortably to provide for their families, is now generally engrossed by one great farmer. One farms an estate of a thousand [pounds] a year, which formerly maintained ten or twenty [families]. Everyone of these little farmers kept a few swine, with some quantity of poultry;

and, having little money, was glad to send his bacon, or pork, or fowls and eggs to market continually. Hence the markets were plentifully served; and plenty created cheapness. But at present, the great, the gentlemen-farmers are above attending to these little things. They breed no poultry or swine, unless for their own use; consequently they send none to market (Wesley 1996, I.6).

As Wesley highlights, the monopolization of farmland into privately owned estates not only prohibited people from farming arable land for their own nourishment but, because this change focused on the production of commodities, it reduced the amount of food available for sale at the local market (Wesley 1996, I.6, I.5).

As we would expect, many of Wesley's criticisms of the food system addressed circumstances pertaining specifically to his time and location. Yet, these circumstances resemble some situations in the current US food system. The US rests on some of the richest agricultural land in the world. Yet despite the promises that industrial agriculture would feed us abundantly and inexpensively, seventeen million people in the US struggled to feed themselves and their families at some point during 2022 (Burroughs 2022, 197–206; USDA 2023). This massive group of people is considered "food insecure," and perhaps surprisingly this number greatly increased *after* the Covid-19 pandemic. The escalating prices of food, inflation, and the end of pandemic-related forms of governmental support have coalesced to increase the numbers of individuals and families experiencing hunger in the US (Khalil 2023). Although the US arguably produces enough food for all living within its borders, it appears that millions of its people face a "scarcity of provisions." Unfortunately, this is the case in many parts of the world today (Burroughs 2022, 241–249).

Much of today's food insecurity arises from the earliest foundations of the United States. The question of who has access to arable land reveals cracks in those foundations. The leaders of colonial America and the government of the US forced indigenous peoples off productive and desirable lands and herded them like cattle onto marginal, less fertile lands. Along with confiscating land, Americans forcibly imported, bought, and sold millions of African people who were enslaved as farm laborers. Even after African Americans were freed and could work land as sharecroppers or landowners, local policies and pressures—including inflated prices for suboptimal agricultural lands, "forced sales, discrimination in agricultural programs, and outright racism"—disproportionately compelled African Americans off farmland and out of farm ownership (King et al. 2018, 682). Additionally, after the Civil War, discriminatory policies and practices convinced (or forced) most landowners of African descent to sell their land. Between 1920 and 2000, "the number of Black farms . . . declined by 98 percent, compared to a 66 percent decline for whites" (King et al. 2018, 682). Black farmers who had once rented or owned land were cut off from their sources of wealth and food, and they were consigned to factory jobs in major city centers (Eberhart 2017, 63). Some of the cities that welcomed them eventually established zoning policies and economic practices that discouraged grocery stores and farmers' markets from serving predominantly Black and Brown communities (Green 2016; Burroughs 2022, 245–47). These and other legacies of injustice live on in the food apartheid many African Americans, tribal citizens, and other marginalized peoples experience every day in our food system. Despite all the injustices, however, some Black and indigenous communities are using their resources and wisdom to establish their own food networks (White 2018; Penniman 2018).

In addition to the injustices that have forced indigenous and Black people off fertile land, economic and political pressures have supported the growth of farm monopolies and a decline in small-scale farms. Since the 1940s, small-scale farmers have been pressured to expand their acreage and concentrate on a couple of commodity crops or animal products. Agronomists have encouraged farmers to buy high-priced seeds, chemicals, and specialized machinery in order to increase income and productivity. Yet, because these expenses are high, and income for products relatively low, farmers struggle to make a living wage, let alone a profit. This causes many small-scale farmers to leave their businesses. Furthermore, since they sell nearly all their products to agribusinesses and food processors, farming families do not directly eat much, if any, of the food they grow. Even if they have the income to buy food, their rural locations limit their grocery store options, which leaves farming families (and their rural neighbors) alarmingly food insecure (Zenk 2014, 2174).

The scarcity of provisions we encounter today in rural and urban communities involves not only land tenure—as Wesley reminds us—but also waste. Some scholars estimate that nearly half of the food grown in the US is wasted at some point along the winding path from field to factory, to grocery store, to fridge, to table. Across the agricultural and food sector, the US "wastes 133 billion pounds of food each year, more than enough to feed the 50 million Americans who regularly face hunger" (Montgomery 2017, 38). Our current food system and food practices sustain this inordinate amount of waste. As a result, food swells our landfills, farming overtaxes our soil and water resources, and millions of people still go hungry. When we consider that the US produces plenty of food to feed its citizens, we can see that the "present scarcity of provisions" stems from injustices enmeshed in the food system itself. Simply put, we inequitably distribute food, narrowly concentrate on a few commodity crops, and unjustly limit access to arable land. God's beloved human creatures go without nourishment, and God's dear creation is misused, with its resources hoarded by some to the detriment of others. In this situation, Wesley's theological heirs must speak, write, and act to promote creation-wide flourishing, health, and well-being.

Conclusion

By critically reading Wesley's ecological interpretations of Scripture, science, and society, we may be inspired to reconsider God's creation-wide work of liberation and, consequently, hone our speaking, writing, and acting so that they more accurately reflect this liberation. Wesley's writings function as an instructive dialogue partner for us as we develop a more ecologically sound hermeneutic by which we interpret Scripture and the world. His hermeneutic remarkably bears the signs of attentiveness to the nonhuman world around him and a willingness to consider that God not only cares for humanity but nonhuman creation. If we allow Wesley's hermeneutic to refocus our attention when we read Scripture and reflect on our experiences of life, we will more likely recognize that the whole of creation receives God's grace, justice, and salvation. What's more, such a hermeneutic allows us to perceive the intricate web of relationships God has established between and among God's creation and Godself.

When we hone our interpretive sensibilities (i.e., our hermeneutic) we will, in turn, adjust and clarify our theologies and ethical convictions. The opposite inevitably happens as well: our theological and ethical convictions inform our hermeneutic. It is, consequently, illuminating to discern what may have been Wesley's ecologically informed theological and ethical convictions communicated in these three texts. These convictions can provide a broad theological and ethical framework for us as we proceed in the back-and-forth movement between interpretation and theological reflection.

Wesley's three works reviewed in this chapter highlight at least six elements of a Wesleyan eco-theological interpretive framework: (1) God actively and lovingly cares and provides for all of creation; (2) human actions affect the health and well-being of the rest of creation; (3) God intends for all people (and, arguably, all nonhuman creatures) to have access to nourishing foods; (4) ecosystems move toward balance and harmony unless disturbed; (5) God is committed to restorative justice; and (6) God ultimately will liberate human and nonhuman creation. These six elements remind us to interpret Scripture, science, society, and countless other facets of our world in more ecologically attuned ways. They may also assist us as we develop our theological and ethical responses to the myriad ecological crises crying out for our attention.

When we recall that God continually cares for creation and provides nourishment for living things (element 1), our minds and hearts perceive the theological importance of food and water. Wesley's theocentric perspective challenges us to reframe our understanding of the natural world so that we no longer think of the water cycle and food chain only in terms of natural law, chance, and human effort. This change of perspective enables us to recognize deforestation (which is deleterious to the water cycle) and the elimination of native plant species (which interrupts the food chain) as working against God's own creative efforts in the world. Similarly, the ways in which industries and farms release pollution into waterways will appear as desecrations of divine blessings. We may also begin to view some farm and city practices of drawing disproportionate amounts of water from rivers and aquifers as unjust forms of hoarding God's blessings, gifts meant to be shared with current and future generations of earth's communities (element 3).

When a few regions or people hoard the blessings of water and abundant plant-life (contra element 2), many of God's beloved creatures—including humans—face hunger, malnutrition, and starvation (element 3). Just as in Wesley's day, our world's current economies, luxuries, land tenure policies, and industries prevent certain groups of people from accessing the sources of life and nourishment. They simultaneously empower other groups to stockpile God's gifts. Such situations work against God's life-sustaining purposes and undermine Wesley's assumption that all people should be able to feed themselves and their families with reasonable effort.

A Wesleyan eco-theological and ethical framework supports us in advocating for all communities—rural, urban, rich, poor, black, brown, white—so that all have equitable access to healthy, nourishing, affordable, and culturally appropriate foods and the land that can produce these foods (elements 3 and 5). It also prompts individuals and communities to reduce their waste of food and resist the impulses of self-gratification and luxury so that everyone has the food and fresh water they need. Christians in the Wesleyan tradition have the opportunity and perhaps even the responsibility to use their powers of influence, like Wesley, to ensure no one goes hungry or thirsty. This Wesleyan concern about nourishment aligns precisely with God's own concern, which a Wesleyan eco-theological hermeneutic reveals.

Yet, even as we pursue providing enough food for everyone, we must promote the balance and harmony God intends for the entire creation since we know human activity can fundamentally alter ecosystems and destroy their balance (element 4), as Wesley himself recognized. According to Wesley, God designed each ecosystem to move towards a balance between consumption and production, destruction of life and renewal of life. As we implement a Wesleyan view of creation, we must seek not only to understand Scripture but also—through scientific means—the relationships between living and nonliving things in undisturbed ecosystems and attempt to mimic them in our own, comparable ecosystems. Attempting to live within the constraints of our home ecosystem requires collaborations between scientists, farmers, economists, urban planners, social scientists, educators, politicians, food service workers, manufacturers, consumers, religious leaders, and countless others, especially in this time of globalization. Our Wesleyan pursuit of an equitable and flourishing society demands holistic, multifaceted perspectives. Inspired by a Wesleyan theological framework and hermeneutic, we as educators, preachers, and Wesleyan Christians can mobilize our congregations to apply their Wesleyan values to every facet of their so-called "private" and "professional" lives and always to do so with humility and courage.

If the complexity of the world is insufficient to inspire humility, Wesley's belief in God's judgment should. While we may be inclined to think that our diminishing or destroying of God's blessings in creation goes mostly unnoticed, Wesley would remind us that the loving Creator is also God the Judge who sees. Wesley's "The General Deliverance" encourages us, nevertheless, to view God the Judge as engaged in restorative justice (element 5) rather than punitive justice. Accordingly, God takes account of the injustices committed against creatures (human as well as nonhuman) in this age and provides reparations for those injustices in the new creation. As we intentionally align ourselves with creation's Judge in the boardroom, at the factory, in the field and forest, in the home, and in the sanctuary, we may—like Wesley—have greater courage to stand against injustice and destruction and instead work toward the equitable sharing of God's blessings. And even when injustice appears to win the day, we may take comfort in the conviction that creation indeed has an attentive and prevailing Advocate.

Momentary losses and setbacks in the struggle for a harmonious and flourishing creation do not undermine the Wesleyan belief in God's ultimate success. As Wesley reminds us, creation's Advocate and Judge not only perceives creation's sufferings and injustices but also has acted in Jesus Christ and continues to act by the Spirit to liberate it (element 6). While much of our preaching and teaching today focuses almost exclusively on God's salvation of humanity, Wesley's soteriology corrects our narrow-mindedness. Salvation extends beyond humanity to include and incorporate all of creation. Does our teaching and preaching claim this as well?

Since God's creation-wide salvation and liberation illustrate God's commitment to and deep valuing of the entire creation, we—as inheritors of the Christian gospel and the Wesleyan eco-theological interpretive framework—have the privilege and responsibility to consider how our individual and corporate lives either collaborate with or momentarily thwart the Creator's salvific aims for all creation. When we allow our hearts and minds to remain permeable to God's truth as it is communicated through Scripture and through the non-human creation, our Wesleyan eco-theological hermeneutic will enable us to approximate the new creation God has in store for the whole creation.

References

Burroughs, Presian Renee. 2022. *Creation's Slavery & Liberation: Paul's Letter to Rome in the Face of Imperial & Industrial Agriculture*. Cascade Library of Pauline Studies. Eugene, OR: Cascade Books.

———. 2021. "A Wesleyan Ecological Hermeneutic: Interpreting Scripture, Science, and Society Ecologically." *Wesleyan Theological Journal* 56, no. 2: 37–56.

Eberhart, Timothy Reinhold. 2017. *Rooted and Grounded in Love: Holy Communion for the Whole Creation*. Distinguished Dissertations in Christian Theology, vol. 14. Eugene, OR: Pickwick Publications.

Fairlie, Simon. 2009. "A Short History of Enclosure in Britain: How Our Land Was Privatized over Five Centuries." *The Land: An Occasional Magazine about Land Rights* 7 (Summer). https://www.thelandmagazine.org.uk/articles/short-history-enclosure-britain.

Green, Clara, ed. 2016. *U.S. Household Food Security: Statistics and Analysis for 2014*. New York: Nova.

Khalil, Ashraf. 2023. "Food Insecurity Shot up Last Year with Inflation and the End of Pandemic-Era Aid, a New Report Says." PBS NewsHour, October 25, 2023. https://www.pbs.org/newshour/economy/food-insecurity-shot-up-last-year-with-inflation-and-the-end-of-pandemic-era-aid-a-new-report-says.

King, Katrina Quisumbing, Spencer D. Wood, Jess Gilbert, and Marilyn Sinkewicz. 2018. "Black Agrarianism: The Significance of African American Landownership in the Rural South." *Rural Sociology* 83, no. 3: 677–99.

Montgomery, David R. 2017. *Growing a Revolution: Bringing Our Soil Back to Life*. New York: W. W. Norton & Company.

Penniman, Leah. 2018. *Farming While Black: Soul Fire Farm's Practical Guide to Liberation on the Land*. White River Junction, VT: Chelsea Green.

USDA 2023. "Food Security in the U.S.: Interactive Charts and Highlights." Last modified October 25, 2023. https://www.ers.usda.gov/topics/food-nutrition-assistance/food-security-in-the-u-s/interactive-charts-and-highlights/#trends.

Wesley, John. 1770. *A Survey of the Wisdom of God in the Creation: Or a Compendium of Natural Philosophy.* Reprint. Second Edition. 5 vols. Bristol: William Pine.

———(1773) 1996. "Thoughts on the Present Scarcity of Provisions." Reprint. In *The Works of John Wesley: Thoughts, Addresses, Prayers, Letters*, vol 11. Albany, OR: Books for the Ages.

———1810. *A Survey of the Wisdom of God in the Creation: A Compendium of Natural Philosophy in Two Volumes.* Lancaster, PA: William Hamilton.

——— 1999. "The General Deliverance" (Sermon 60). The Sermons of John Wesley. Nampa, ID: Wesley Center. https://wesley.nnu.edu/john-wesley/the-sermons-of-john-wesley-1872-edition/sermon-60-the-general-deliverance/.

White, Monica M. 2018. *Freedom Farmers: Agricultural Resistance and the Black Freedom Movement.* Chapel Hill: The University of North Carolina Press.

Zenk, Shannon N., et al. 2014. "Relative and Absolute Availability of Healthier Food and Beverage Alternatives across Communities in the United States." *American Journal of Public Health* 104, no. 11: 2170–78.

CHAPTER 4

Reading Samson with Wesleyan Eyes

Stephen Riley

In his sermon "On Sin in Believers" (Sermon 13), John Wesley argues that in the believer, "the evil nature, still remains (although subdued) and wars against the Spirit" (*Works* 1:333). For Wesley and his theological descendants, living faithfully in a relationship with God requires a diligent examination of one's life. Believers are to "watch and pray," as Wesley put it, for the Spirit to search us and expose the ways of life that are antithetical to the ways of Christ. The proper response to exposed sin in our life is repentance, which is a twofold process. The first part is a confession, acknowledging our sins and the sinful state of the world. The second act is calling upon Christ to help us, admitting we cannot, by our power, change the world or ourselves. Repentance understood this way does not just happen once in the believer's life. Instead, the faithful will need to examine their lives, repent, and seek God's help continually. The good news is that God does not leave us on our own. Christ has overcome the power of sin and can help us in the process of healing and becoming whole, or, as Wesley would call it, holiness.

Wesleyans believe Scripture plays an important role in that examination. Through Scripture reading, Wesley believed Christians should seek to know God's will. To accomplish this task, Wesley encouraged his readers always to keep the central doctrines such as original sin, justification by faith, and holiness before them. In doing so, reading Scripture can become a way for the

Spirit to enlighten one to the places where repentance is necessary, and God's grace and help can transform us.

This chapter will explore a reading of the Old Testament (OT) as an act of examination in Wesleyan theology and practice. The Book of Judges belongs to the genre of repentance literature in ancient Israel. As such, the reader should not engage the text primarily as an endorsement of the materials found therein. Instead, it should be read as a confession for what happened and how these choices ultimately resulted in broken relationships and exile from the land. To help, we will begin by examining the OT text of Judges as a whole. We will specifically look at the "Judges Cycle" of sin, oppression, and repentance as a model for reading the book. Then, we will focus on the Samson narrative as an example of how the cycle spins out of control because of the unchecked effects of sin. Next, we will discuss how the text functions as part of Israel's historical literature. In this section, we will explore how the final form of Judges serves the purpose of repentance for failing to remain faithful to God's covenant. Hopefully, it will help us to see how reading the OT offers us a way to live into a key feature of Wesleyan Christianity, namely, examining our lives, engaging in repentance, and experiencing healing.

The Book as a Whole: A Sad Story in Three Movements

If you ask people what primary image of Samson they have, they may respond that he was a strong man calling on God to help him destroy his enemies. This picture comes from an interpretation of the story, formed either by the New Testament (NT) book of Hebrews or modern film that depicts Samson as a hero. This portrait includes a relatively flat set of stories pulled from the biblical text and shaped for our modern sensibilities. We like strong men who defeat enemies. We want love stories, such as the ones portrayed in movies, so we elevate part of the narrative about Samson and Delilah. However, a closer reading of Judges as an example of repentance shows that the story is much more complex. It becomes clear that Samson is not the hero of the narrative and is, rather, an antihero for Israel. To understand this claim, however, one must recognize how the Samson story fits within the Book of Judges and closely read the entire Samson story.

Judges 13:1–16:35 contains the Samson narrative. The story comes right after a failed attempt to set up a kingship by Abimelech and the rash vow of Jephthah. It is followed by the terrible news of the Levite and his concubine and civil war in Israel. Within the four chapters is a set of shorter descriptions about a local hero and explanation stories about places from the tribe of Dan. The present form of these narratives reflects a complex history of development. The general scholarly consensus is that the Book of Judges probably represents three stages of development within which the Samson narratives fit. First, there were the local independent stories that would have circulated to recount military leaders and their exploits. Second, these local traditions would have been collected into some form of the Book of Judges that would have highlighted a period in Israel's past and its various local leaders who helped Israel through a particular time in their history. Finally, the book would have been edited into a form included in what is commonly called the Deuteronomistic History.

The Deuteronomistic History would have served the needs of Jerusalem leaders who were returning from the exile in 539 BCE. This history attempts to explain, in terms consistent with the political and theological views expressed in Deuteronomy, the development of the monarchy and eventual destruction of Jerusalem in 586 BCE. In this final state, two critical factors are added. First, chapter 1 was most likely added to Judges as a prologue that gives a very different picture of the conquest of the Promised Land from that in the Book of Joshua. This introduction set the scene for the following cycle that will play out throughout the book and end with the words, "In those days there was no king in Israel; all the people did what was right in their own eyes" (17:6). The book essentially becomes a bridge between the leadership of Joshua and the beginning of the monarchy traditions found in the Book of Samuel. Second, the historian framed the stories of the judges with what is commonly called the Judges Cycle. This cycle is laid out in Judges 2:11-18 and sets a pattern to evaluate Israel's judge. The cycle states:

1. Israel does evil in the eyes of YHWH

2. YHWH hands them over to their oppressors for a certain number of years

3. Israel cries out for deliverance

4. YHWH hears their cries and raises up a judge
5. The judge delivers Israel from their oppressor
6. (at this point, there may or may not be a story about the deliverance)
7. After the judge dies, Israel once again does evil in the eyes of YHWH

The stories that appear in the book follow this pattern. However, as biblical scholars notice, only a couple of the judges fully follow this pattern. As the narrative continues, more and more pieces of the cycle go missing as Israel falls deeper into the abyss of sin and apostasy until there is no judge by the end of the book. In fact, at the end of the book, the reader is confronted by horror after horror as sexual abuse, wanton destruction, and blatant disregard for human life become the hallmarks of each story. The final refrain in Judges 21:25, "In those days there was no king in Israel; each person did what was right in their own eyes" repeats in the final chapters. As a judgment on Israel, the refrain not only sets up the movement toward Israel's monarchy but it also highlights the chaos and brokenness found in Israel at that time. The Samson narrative is found at a significant moment within the spiral toward chaos.

Movement 1: The Miraculous Birth Gone Awry

In its present form, there are three movements to the Samson narrative. The first movement occurs in chapter 13, which begins with the note, "The Israelites again did what was evil did in the sight of the LORD and the LORD gave them into the hand of the Philistines forty years. Although this sets the reader up to believe the cycle of repentance will continue, the story stops following the cycle at this point. There is no clear point where Israel cries out to YHWH for deliverance, and rest for the land will ultimately be difficult to find. However, in this first movement, it does appear that the LORD might be raising up a deliverer.

This first movement is divided into two parts. The first part of the narrative is primarily the story of a miraculous birth. In this part of the story, a messenger of the LORD tells an unnamed woman that she will bear a child who will be a Nazarite. This Nazarite child, a person who never eats or drinks anything unclean or never has a razor touch his head, will deliver Israel from the Philistines. The whole episode is fraught with mystery and anxiety, but it leaves us hopeful of the possibilities for what a miracle child could do to deliver Israel. However, it does not take long for the narrative to reveal that this miracle child will not fulfill our hopes. Instead, he will become a man-child that exploits opportunities for self-fulfillment and violent tendencies.

The second part of this first movement occurs in 14:1–15:8a and centers on Samson's wedding in Timnah, a Philistine city. In this story, we begin to see Samson's true character and the result of the ongoing downward spiral of unchecked sin and destruction. Samson goes to Timnah and desires to marry a foreign woman, which was tantamount to apostasy according to the theology that influenced the Book of Judges. At his wedding feast, Samson makes and loses a bet with some of the local rulers. We, the readers of the story, know he loses because his wife pressured him to give her the answer. We also know that the same local rulers who made the bet with Samson were intimidating his wife, forcing her to get the answer from Samson. However, in the story's world, Samson does not know any of this and, upon losing the bet, he goes to a nearby town and kills thirty people to pay his debt. After paying his debt to the local rulers, Samson leaves Timnah in anger and abandons his wife. The next thing we read about is how Samson returns to Timnah to find his wife married to one of the men to whom he'd lost the bet. This prompts Samson to burn Timnah's fields with foxes he set on fire. The cycle of revenge is not over, however. In response to the loss of their fields, the people of Timnah decide to burn to death Samson's former wife and father-in-law. One of the last things we read is Samson saying, "If this is how you act, then I won't stop until I get revenge on you!" (15:7 CEB) and then proceeding to strike them with more violence. The entire first movement spirals out of control from promise of possibility to revenge in a matter of a few verses.

Movement 2: Broken Relationships

In the narratives that follow, Samson's story continues this violence. Samson finds himself in story after story of destructive brokenness. First, he is surrounded at a cave in Etam. Both Philistines and Israelites are involved as both groups desire Samson's surrender and an end to the cycle of revenge. However, as Samson is handed over to the Philistines, we read, "the spirit of the LORD rushed upon him" (15:14). This phrase, or some form of it occurred earlier in the story. It was mention in chapter 13 at Samson's birth, in 14:6, when Samson killed the lion, and in 14:19, when Samson went down to Ashkelon to kill the thirty men to get garments to repay his gambling debt. In these instances, the Spirit of YHWH appears to mark Samson in a special way or empowers him to complete feats of strength. However, the narrator does not clearly state that Spirit of YHWH is empowering Samson to act as a judge for Israel. In 15:18-20, an etiology is given for the location of a well in Lehi, the same place in the previous etiology. In this story, Samson is thirsty and asks YHWH to give him a drink. YHWH opens up a drinking spot in Lehi and that place is called En-hakkore, which in Hebrew means "spring of the one who calls out." This section ends with a note that Samson judged Israel for twenty years. This is a likely end to the narratives about Samson, which at one point that would have matched the Judges Cycle. There is no rest or peace for Israel, however, and the story is not over yet.

Movement 3: Destroying Our Enemy?

As the third movement begins, the focus of the narrative turns back to Samson's engagement with women. In this section of the text, two women play a prominent role. First, there is a short story about a sexual encounter Samson has with an unnamed Philistine prostitute from Gaza. As he is spending the night with this woman, word of Samson's presence gets out, the people surround him and attempt to apprehend him in an allusion to the earlier story of the cave. In this story, Samson sneaks out, tears the gates off the city wall, and carries them back toward Hebron in an apparent rebuke of the people trying to catch him.

Next, we encounter a more familiar narrative from the Samson cycle. In this story, we read that Samson loved the woman named Delilah. However, we are also told the rulers of the Philistines are pushing her to help them to finally get Samson. In allusion to the earlier Timnah story, Samson is pestered into giving away an answer that costs him. This time, Delilah asks Samson about the source of his strength. She asks three times and, each time, Samson tells her something that doesn't work. Each time, Delilah has an ambush of Philistine soldiers waiting nearby and each time, Samson emerges from the trap victorious. This small cycle would be comical if it were not for what happens next. Finally, Delilah returns and asks him to reveal his secret. When he does, the text informs us that she knows he has been truthful. In agonizing textual time, verses 17-22 tell us that the Philistines got their revenge and brought Samson, blinded and weak, down into the grinding mills of Gaza.

The story turns once more and ends with a festival with all the Philistines celebrating Samson's capture and their god, Dagon, and his victory over Samson. The celebration is highlighted by the Philistines calling to have Samson perform for them. At some point during the performance, Samson is placed between the two pillars that apparently hold up the entire temple. In one last act of revenge, Samson prays, "LORD God, please remember me! Make me strong just this once more, God, so I can have revenge on the Philistines, just one act of revenge for my two eyes" (16:28 CEB). The final notes about Samson focus on the number of people he had killed and that he had led Israel for twenty years.

That is the end of the Samson cycle. There is no note that Israel ever called out to God during their oppression. There is no clear sense that Samson actually delivered Israel from the Philistines or any other group. Instead, one could argue that Samson's love of Philistine women entraps him and keeps him from fulfilling the promise his birth story offers. In the end, there is no note that Samson brought about rest for the land. Moreover, the following stories in Judges suggest that instead of repentance, Israel progresses into unspeakable violence and unchecked chaos. Rather than bringing deliverance, Samson accelerated Israel's self-destruction.

Judges as Part of Israel's History

In order to understand the Samson story fully, it is important to place it within its literary and historical contexts. Samson's narrative belongs to the Book of Judges, which in turn belongs to part of our canon that retells Israel's past from the standpoint of their exilic experience. The books of Joshua, Judges, Samuel, and Kings are shaped in a way to help explain Israel's experience of entering, living in, and then losing the Promised Land. A significant question of the history is whether Israel loves God completely and trusts God to care for them in the Promised Land. As we'll see, the overarching answer of the history is that Israel's leaders did not lead the people in loving God fully. The result was a loss of the Promised Land. Reading it from this perspective, the hoped-for response is that the returning people would learn from their past failures and change their ways in the present reality.

The Book of Joshua

The book of Joshua begins the story with a retelling of how Joshua led the people into the Promised Land. As Joshua does this, he continually asks the people if they will follow the Lord with all their heart. Although their answer is a clear yes, their actions throughout the book reveal how the people have difficulty trusting in God to deliver. Consistently, they choose to take matters into their own hands rather than follow God's directions. At the end of Joshua, the people are asked again to renew their covenant with God and reaffirm their commitment to following the Lord. In an often-quoted verse from the book, Joshua says: "Choose today whom you will serve whether the gods your ancestors served in the region beyond the River or the gods of the Amorites in whose land you are living; but as for me and my household, we will serve the LORD!" (Joshua 24:15). The Israelites reply by affirming their allegiance to God alone. Yet, even with the opportunity to affirm their wholehearted love for God, it is not long before we read in the Book of Judges that the story has quickly gone awry.

The Books of Samuel and Kings

On the other side of Judges are the books of Samuel and Kings. In the books of Samuel, we read about the rise and fall of four significant characters. First, we learn of the fall of the house of Eli, a priest of Shiloh, who allowed his sons to manipulate the people for personal gain. Then we follow the story of Samuel, a boy God called to lead the people and a prophet who later becomes bitter when the Israelites choose to have Saul lead them as their king. Next, we read about the unlikely king, Saul, who is chosen to lead but then is rejected when he doesn't follow God's commands. Finally, we are introduced to David, a shepherd boy who will become a king of great renown. However, on the road to becoming king and while king, David commits more than his share of indiscretions and violence. This way of being comes back to haunt David during the latter part of his reign. In those years, as one of his prophets said to him, it seems that violence never leaves his family. Consistent years of rebellion and war chase David until the end of his life.

The books of Kings begin with the end of David's life and the transfer of power to his son Solomon. Even at the end of his life David is unable to escape the consequences of his family's brokenness as two of his sons believe they are the rightful heir and each one tries to take the throne. In the end, however, Solomon is crowned as king over all Israel. His early reign is particularly positive as he oversees the completion of the Jerusalem temple. The dedication ceremony in 1 Kings 8 is full of language like that found in the Book of Deuteronomy and Joshua's speeches to Israel. In his speech, Solomon calls on Israel to be completely faithful and love God with all their heart. Solomon states that if they fail to follow God's commands, things will go poorly for them, but if they repent and return to God, they will find healing. This is a significant point in the historical narrative. Following this high moment, Solomon's story begins to head in a downward direction. We are told how he engages in practices that lead him from complete loyalty to God and care for Israel. At the end of his narrative, we are told that the kingdom is besieged by several adversaries, both foreign and internal, who will tear the kingdom apart.

After Solomon's death, the united monarchy of Israel is divided into two kingdoms, the north and the south. These two kingdoms' stories are told through the rest of the books of Kings. In these narratives we learn of two kingdoms generally failing to love God faithfully as they were called. We learn of terrible kings who directly oppose the ways of God and bring disaster on the people. There are narratives about ambivalent leaders, those who fail to actively pursue the right course of action and therefore lead people astray, and there are some narratives about righteous kings, those who seek God and attempt to lead the people in pursuit of faithful love of God's covenant. One aspect of the narratives about the kings who are righteous is their willingness to humble themselves and repent in the face of unfaithfulness and sin. However, the historian points to the destruction of both kingdoms as evidence neither one truly returned to God. In 2 Kings 17, the historian explains the destruction of the northern kingdom in terms of a failure to love God fully and a failure to repent of their wrongs. Later, the southern kingdom is led by two kings, Hezekiah and Josiah, who lead times of revival in Jerusalem. However, neither one can ultimately deliver the people. The last few chapters of 2 Kings recount how the Babylonians, in 586 BCE, completed their siege of Jerusalem by looting the temple and burning it to the ground.

The History of Israel as Repentance Literature

The telling of Israel's history is designed to help make sense of the outcome of exile in Babylon. When Israel finds itself in a foreign land, defeated by a people who claim that their god gave them victory in battle, Israel was forced to explain what had happened. One of the possible interpretations of the history as a whole then was that Israel failed, not God. In the ancient world, a common way of thinking about war and its outcome was to believe that the victorious army's god was the more powerful god. In these circumstances, a result was for the losing side to believe their god had either abandoned them or was simply a lesser god in the ancient world.

What Israel seems to have done, however, is to interpret their history through a different lens, one that is significantly important for us as modern readers. Instead of accepting that their god was somehow less powerful than the god of Babylon, Israel reviewed their history through the lens of the covenant that God made with Israel upon entering the Promised Land. Part of that covenant was for Israel to remain completely loyal to God's commandments, especially to serve and worship God alone. Part of the story highlights the ways in which Israel's leadership especially fails in the task of aiding people ultimately to accomplish this task. In the end, what we are left with is not a chronicle of Israel's increasing victory, as we do in other ancient Near Eastern texts or even what we find in the books of 1 and 2 Chronicles, but a national confession.

Reading the Text with Wesleyan Eyes

Considering these things, one might ask, "What are we supposed to do?" As Wesleyans we believe God is reaching out in love for our redemption. As Wesley encouraged his followers, we also believe that Scripture is a means of ensuring that we encounter the grace of God necessary for our salvation. If we are to examine our life on the journey of faith in order to bring to light anything that might be antithetical to the ways of God and repent of it, one way we might read the Samson story is through a similar lens, looking back just as Israel did from exile. Instead of reading it as a hero text, as some people do, or as a model of faith, which is what one chapter in the New Testament does, we might consider the whole story as an opportunity to see in ourselves actions and attitudes that need confession and the grace of God to change.

Example 1: The Birth Story and Trusting God

As we think about reading the text in this way, we might begin by looking at the story of Samson's birth. In that story, Samson's mother encounters a messenger of God who tells her she will conceive a child. An important point to know about this part of the story is that Samson's mother was barren. In the ancient world, being barren was especially problematic, because it was thought to signify that something was wrong between the woman and the divine. However, notice that Samson's mother believes the messenger; and it is Manoah, Samson's father, who struggles to believe the message. As we examine our lives, we might consider this story and ask how we are trusting in God on the journey of faith. In Wesley's sermons a considerable refrain is "by faith," whether that be in talking about justification or sanctification. Thus, we might consider how we are doing, in terms of trusting God daily. Do we, like the unnamed mother, reflect the trusting faith or are we more like Manoah, who is unable to believe until he sees some spectacular event. In the narrative, Manoah is not entirely rejected for his lack of belief in the message. He is, however, highlighted as one who did not trust in the divine messenger.

I wonder if, in the evaluation of our journey, we often fall into what are known as "false dichotomies," that is, either/or thinking. We believe we've either gotten it right or wrong. However, in this first narrative in the Samson story we are offered two models of response to consider. As we read, we can examine our life before God and recognize that there are times when we do trust God's work in our life and times when we don't. If we believe that God is working for our good because God loves us, then we can repent of the times we don't trust and then lean on God for help in the future.

Example 2: Rashness, Broken Relationships, and Unrepentance

Another way we interpret the Samson story to examine our life could be to look at the second movement in the story and note the way in which our life intersects with the lives of others. In the second movement, remember, Samson's story moves toward Timnah and cities of the Philistines. There, Samson's life, which was promised to God as a Nazarite, veers into relationships and ways of being the result in violence and revenge. As we read, we might consider the ways of our own life.

Wesley strongly encouraged his followers to seek out the grace of God that leads to holiness and sanctification. We believe that sanctification looks like holy love lived out in the ways of the Spirit: love, joy, peace, patience, kindness, goodness, faithfulness, gentleness, and self-control. When we see in ourselves actions and attitudes that are antithetical to these ways, we should confess them, seek forgiveness, and ask God for the grace to grow into a new way of life. As Samson, understood here as an antihero, exemplifies rash decisions, violent revenge, and the inability to bring deliverance for Israel, it seems that the storytellers are highlighting that part of the reason Israel ended up in exile was that their leaders failed to follow God's direction. We might, therefore, read these stories as ways to examine what outcomes may result from our failures to live into the way of life that God desires for us. Wesley would point out that the consequences of sin can include loss of fellowship with God and neighbor. Much as Samson found himself surrounded by both Israelites and Philistines alike because of his violent behavior, perhaps our own actions have driven us to separation from God and others. The opportunity we have as we read the text is to learn from

Samson's fatal flaws. Unlike Samson, who never repents or seeks to change, we can participate in the process of examination and repentance as Wesley would define it.

Example 3: Destroying Our Enemies?

A final example we can look at comes from the third movement in the Samson story. In this section, the Samson story turns particularly to focus on Samson's relationship with Delilah and the Philistines. While this story is often portrayed as a love story in the movies, in the text their relationship is complex because Samson is a Nazarite and Delilah is a foreign woman. Adding to the intrigue is the fact that Delilah is working with, and perhaps being pressured by, the Philistine rulers. This part of the story mirrors an earlier part of Samson's story where Samson's first wife manipulated him to give away the answer to his riddle because she was being pressured by the local rulers. This story trades on what is a common feature in the ancient world and is part of ancient Israelite literature: the insider/outsider problem.

For ancient peoples, who were often tribal in nature, people outside their group were to be feared. Israel was no different and their literature often reflects this perspective. In various texts in the OT there are aspects of Israel's national defense, as it might be called, in which the text claims a sort of desire to see a non-Israelite demoted, humiliated, defeated, or otherwise erased from Israel's story. However, it seems that in the exile Israel was confronted with the reality of non-Israelites who were not necessarily to be feared. The evidence can be found in texts like Ruth and Jonah, where foreigners respond favorably to God and God responds graciously to them. Thus, as the end of Samson's story spins toward its conclusion, we might see it not as much as a justification of religious violence or hypersexual prowess, but as judgment. One can then take notice of Samson's last lines and see not a prayer for God's help to save Israel but an abuse of the role of judge to take revenge one last time, "Just one act of revenge for my two eyes!" Even the narrator can only say, "So those he killed at his death were more than those he had killed during his life," and "He had judged Israel twenty years." At the end of Samson's story there is no deliverance and no rest for the land.

The Judges Cycle that was set up at the beginning of the book has not been followed and what we are left with is a sad ending to this story. However, as Wesleyans reading Samson's story, we are not left without the opportunity to engage it for our examination. One of the things we might ask ourselves is: How are we participating in ways of life that lead toward the destruction of people who look like enemies? If Israel learned from their failure and their exile that not all non-Israelites are enemies to be feared and not all foreign women will lead you to worship other gods, then perhaps this last movement of Samson's story offers us an opportunity to reflect on the ways in which we set up false enemies and render certain members of society as "tempters" that will lead us away from the path of God. By creating this theology of fear, we fail to see the image of God in people who are not us. Perhaps, by reading the Samson narrative as repentance literature, we can begin to see the "other," whoever that group or person may be in our life, as someone not to be conquered but as someone created in the image of God and who deserves the opportunity to grow and flourish and journey with God.

Sanctification and holiness are the process whereby we are continually renewed in the image of God and, as Wesleyans, we believe that renewal allows us to love our enemies. By examining ourselves in light of this story and engaging in the process of repentance, perhaps we can name our enemies and begin the process of healing as we journey toward wholeness through God's grace.

Conclusion

In this chapter, I attempted to show how the Samson story functioned within a portion of Israel's historical literature as a repentance text. As such, I also tried to show how we as Wesleyans can read the text today in a similar fashion, seeking to examine our own life for areas where our actions and attitudes are consistent with God's ways. The Samson story is not an endorsement of violence, revenge, and other harmful behaviors. Instead, from the exile, Israel recognized that Samson's behavior contributed to the downward spiral that led to the destruction of Jerusalem and the forced migration to Babylon. For contemporary Wesleyans, our goal in reading the text should be to see how our way of life fails to reflect the holy love of God in the world.

The Samson story offers significant opportunity to examine our life in order to see ways in which we mirror Samson's brokenness. When the Spirit of God reveals things to us through such a reading of the text, we should then engage in the practice of repentance, confession and turning to God.

For Further Reading

Chretain Erickson, Diandra. 2018. "Judges." In *Postcolonial Commentary and the Old Testament*, edited by Hemchand Gossai, 122–46. London: Bloomsbury.

Heller, Roy L. 2011. *Conversations with Scripture: The Book of Judges*. Anglican Association of Biblical Scholars Study Series. New York: Morehouse.

Janzen, David. 2020. 'The Deuteronomistic History as Literature of Trauma." In *The Oxford Handbook of the Historical Books of the Hebrew Bible*, edited by Brad E. Kelle and Brent A. Strawn, 421–33. New York: Oxford University Press.

Jost, Renate. 1999. "God of Love/God of Vengeance, Or Samson's 'Prayer for Vengeance.'" In *A Feminist Companion to Judges*, edited by Athalya Brenner. A Feminist Companion to the Bible (Second Series), 117–25. Sheffield: Sheffield Academic Press.

Seibert, E. A. 2009. *Disturbing Divine Behavior: Troubling Old Testament Images of God*. Minneapolis: Fortress Press.

Wesley, John. 1984. "On Sin in Believers" (Sermon 13). In *Sermons I 1–33*. Edited by Albert C. Outler. Vol. 1 of *The Bicentennial Editions of the Works of John Wesley*, edited by Albert Outler et al. 317–34. Nashville: Abingdon Press.

Yee, Gale A. 1995. *Judges and Method: New Approaches in Biblical Studies*. Minneapolis: Fortress Press.

CHAPTER 5

God of Mercy, God of Wrath
Reading the Hard Parts of Scripture with the Early Church

Charles Rivera

In the Book of Exodus, after the incident of the golden calf, God instructs Moses to ascend Mount Sinai once again to make new stone tablets to replace the original ones, which Moses had broken upon seeing Israel's apostasy at the foot of the mountain. Once Moses has hewn the new tablets and returned to the height of the mountain, God descends in a cloud and declares himself:

> "The LORD, the LORD,
> a God merciful and gracious,
> slow to anger,
> and abounding in steadfast love and faithfulness,
> keeping steadfast love for the thousandth generation,
> forgiving iniquity and transgression and sin
> yet by no means clearing the guilty,
> but visiting the iniquity of the parents
> upon the children
> and the children's children,
> to the third and the fourth generation."
> —Exodus 34:6-7

These verses, coming at a climactic moment in the story of Exodus, are one of the clearest summaries in all of Scripture of the character of God. God self-identifies as "the LORD," YHWH, not God in the abstract but the God of Abraham, Isaac, and Jacob—God, who appeared to Moses in the burning bush and brought his people out of Egypt. Next, God's self-descriptions increase in their detail. First of all, the LORD is "merciful and gracious." Then elaborating a bit further, we find that God is "slow to anger," meaning that God chooses patience over flying into a rage. The LORD is also "abounding in steadfast love and faithfulness," meaning that God does not swerve from love or fail to fulfill promises. Finally, God becomes even more concrete: God's love and faithfulness extend "to the thousandth generation," which in biblical idiom effectively means forever.[1] The LORD's forgiveness covers "iniquity and transgression and sin"—in other words, not just certain things, but all sorts of offenses and wrongdoings committed against God.

At this moment in the story of Exodus, Moses has seen firsthand the grace and faithfulness of God: when Israel turned away to worship the Golden Calf, God chose not to destroy them but to show mercy and keep to the promises made to them. And yet, God's self-declaration does not end there. Although these descriptions begin with mercy and grace, they conclude by affirming God's justice or righteousness. The LORD does not "clear the guilty." In other words, forgiveness here does not mean that God simply ignores wrongdoing or treats it as though it were inconsequential. Far from being untroubled by injustice, the LORD extends punishment of iniquity for several generations. This punishment does not go on forever, the way God's steadfast love does, but three or four generations is certainly enough time to get the point across: God may be slow to anger, but God is not content to let the wicked run wild. In the course of Exodus, Moses had seen divine justice too, above all when God punished Pharaoh for

---

1. This sentiment is like Jesus's answer to Peter that his followers should forgive "not just seven times, but rather as many as seventy-seven times" (Matt. 18:21-22). Just as one would hardly imagine that Jesus instructs Peter meticulously to record the number of times he has forgiven in order to begin to hold a grudge after the seventy-seventh instance, so also one should not imagine that, when the clock strikes midnight on the thousandth generation, God's steadfast love turns into a pumpkin.

oppressing and exploiting the Israelites and continually going back on his promises to let them go.

These verses from Exodus can be very confusing. They can feel like whiplash. First God forgives everything, but then God also does not clear the guilty? God's love extends from generation to generation, but then we read that God's punishments extend from generation to generation too? God claims to be merciful and gracious, but then the LORD visits the iniquity of the parents upon their children. For many readers of the Bible, it might almost seem like there are two different Gods here: one who is merciful and forgiving and another who is wrathful and exacting.

This sense that there are two different gods is not limited to this one passage in Exodus. For many Christians, this whiplash extends throughout the whole Bible. In popular terms it often goes something like this: "The God of the Old Testament is all wrath and judgment, but the God of the New Testament is all love and forgiveness." Some people might say that Jesus's teachings of love were meant to lead us away from the teachings of the Old Testament (OT)—some might even say that Jesus's death on the cross delivered us from the punishment of the wrathful Old Testament God. Others would say that it is not so much that God has changed, but that people's perceptions of God have changed: in the world of the OT, they imagined God as angry and judgmental, but by the New Testament (NT), because of Jesus, people realized that God was merciful and loving.

Whatever version of these popular ideas we take, they agree on this distinction between the wrathful God of the OT and the loving God of the NT. Yet we can see, just from this passage in Exodus, that this does not really hold up. Exodus is in the OT, yet God is described here as merciful and gracious. God extends punishment "to the third or fourth generation," but extends steadfast love "for the thousandth generation"—forever. This doesn't seem like it is simply the purely wrathful "Old Testament God" of popular belief. We could go to the NT as well and find many instances of God passing judgment, such as Jesus's parables of the foolish bridesmaids, the talents, and the sheep and the goats (Matthew 25). The truth must be a bit more complicated.

So, what do we Wesleyan Christians do when faced with a difficult scriptural challenge like this? Where do we turn to help us make sense of the hard parts of Scripture? Although there are many answers to this question, there is one truth that is always good to keep in mind when facing difficult passages of Scripture: *you are probably not the first person who has struggled to understand them.* People have been reading and struggling with the Scriptures for centuries and centuries. As Wesleyan Christians, we do not believe that we have to figure everything out for ourselves. We do not believe that we have to cut ourselves off from the "so great a cloud of witnesses" (Heb. 12:1) who have gone before us and walk some lonesome valley all by ourselves. As Wesleyan Christians, we are not just willing to learn from our forefathers and foremothers in the Christian faith—we seek them out!

Drawing on the Riches of the Past: Four Views

Although it might seem like common sense to listen to the voices of Christians from previous eras of history, not everybody would agree with the Wesleyan Christian perspective on learning from the great "cloud of witnesses." Some would give various reasons for why we should not listen to the voices of the past or would have a different view on which voices are important. These other Christians might have some good reasons for saying what they do, but they all fall short of the Wesleyan perspective in important ways. Here are three views on listening to Christians of the past that you might commonly encounter among non-Wesleyan Christians.

The Biblicist View

The first is the Biblicist View. A biblicist would discourage Christians from seeking out help from days gone by when presented with a difficult passage in Scripture. A biblicist might say something like, "Only the Bible is the word of God. Only the Bible is authoritative. We should not look to the writings of the past to help us understand the Bible. Those are only human traditions—they're human-made. We should use the Bible to interpret the Bible. We do not need lots of historical knowledge to get to the meaning of God's word. Scripture alone is our guide."

The Modernist View

Another perspective would be the Modernist View. A modernist would also discourage Christians from reading the writings of the past to help them understand Scripture, but for very different reasons than those held by the biblicists. A modernist might say something like, "The best way to understand the Bible is to look at the most modern and up-to-date scholars. You should not read what ancient Christians said because they did not understand the Bible as well as we do. They were very superstitious, but now we are able to study the Bible scientifically. Do not read those earlier Christians—you wouldn't want to be behind the times."

The Traditionalist View

Yet a third perspective would be the Traditionalist View. Unlike the biblicist and the modernist, the traditionalist would *encourage* Christians to dip into the writings of the past to help them understand the Bible as long as they were reading the *right*, that is "orthodox," authors. A traditionalist might say something like, "To understand the Bible, you have to read it within the tradition of the church. There are lots of ways to interpret the Bible and the only way you can be sure you've got it right is by following the creeds of the church and the writings of people who are agreed to be orthodox. In fact, if you read the Bible without these guidelines, you'll almost certainly get it wrong. But you can't just read anyone from the past—if you read people who had the wrong opinions, you'll just get confused. Fortunately, I've got a list here of approved authors you can choose from . . ."

The Wesleyan Christian View

As Wesleyan Christians, we are able to recognize some of the merits of these different views, even if we are also aware of their shortcomings. If we had to pick one, we would probably choose some form of the traditionalist view, but that view does not fully capture our perspective. To see why, consider some of John Wesley's views on this subject.

Like the biblicists, John Wesley emphasized the unique authority of Scripture. He endeavored to be "a man of one book," dedicated to the teaching of the Bible above all else ("On God's Vineyard," Sermon 107, I.1; Maddox 2012, 3–18). But that did not stop him from reading widely and voraciously—and encouraging his preachers to do the same. Wesleyan Christians recognize the merit of exalting Scripture above all other books, but that does not mean we refuse to read widely to help us interpret Scripture. Like the modernists, Wesley saw great value in the biblical scholarship of his contemporaries. However, he did not think it was wise to read only recent writings. Likewise, Wesleyan Christians value the insights of modern scholarship, but that doesn't mean we devalue the insights of past Christians.

Like the traditionalists, John Wesley encouraged the early Methodists to draw on the authors of the past, but he did not limit himself to those authors generally considered orthodox. In fact, Wesley sometimes praised ancient figures, like Montanus or Pelagius, who are generally considered heretics! ("The Wisdom of God's Counsels," Sermon 68, ¶9; Campbell 1991, 76–81). Although he valued doctrinal orthodoxy, what was most important to Wesley was whether their writings could help people lead a life of holiness.[2] Sometimes authors whose writings are perfectly orthodox can be cold and speculative and sometimes authors who inflame the heart with love of God are not perfect in every point of doctrine. John Wesley could also be skeptical of the historical circumstances under which certain authors came to be considered orthodox and others came to be considered heretics.

For example, he suspected that, much like the early Methodists, Montanus and Pelagius got bad reputations because they advocated for a more rigorous Christian discipline, which scandalized the laxer, more respectable members of the church. As Wesley rightly saw, decisions about who is orthodox and who is not can have as much to do with politics and worldly power as the correctness of doctrine ("The Wisdom of God's Counsels," Sermon 68, 9). Wesleyan Christians value doctrinal orthodoxy when consulting the authors of the past, but the pursuit of holiness is even more important. As a result, we do not always subscribe to the lists of who is in and who is out

---

2. See Robert W. Wall, "'The Way of Full Salvation': An Introduction to Wesleyan Biblical Interpretation" chapter 1 in this book.

that other Christians might consider sacrosanct. Wesley himself was ambivalent about the importance of ancient church councils, which many Christian denominations consider definitive on points of doctrine. Nevertheless, he valued the works of the earliest Christians (Campbell 1991, 78–81).

There is one other noteworthy aspect of John Wesley's perspective: he placed great emphasis on what he called "primitive Christianity," by which he meant he meant Christianity characterized by the simplicity and purity of the time of the apostles. He saw the first few centuries of Christian history as especially representative of this primitive Christianity because the church was not yet entangled in all the seductive webs of social and political power. Early in his life, "Primitive Christianity" was even John's nickname among his friends (Campbell 1991, 26–27). Wesley saw the spirit of primitive Christianity and its concern for holiness above all in his favorite authors from the Early Church, like Clement of Alexandria and Macarius the Great. As noted above, Wesley's yearning for primitive Christianity also caused him to view figures like Montanus and Pelagius positively, as people who had fought to maintain the austerity and discipline of the apostolic church against the tides of worldliness already arising in their own day. A vision of "Primitive Christianity" as pure, simple, and united by love, as well as his desire for present Christianity to return to such a state, is memorably expressed in Charles Wesley's poem "Primitive Christianity" which was appended to the second edition of John's *An Earnest Appeal to Men of Reason and Religion*. As Wesleyan Christians, we follow John Wesley's lead in looking back with special reverence to the early centuries of the church, as well as all other times and places that exemplify the spirit of primitive Christianity.

In summary, by following Wesley's practice and example, Wesleyan Christians are eager to draw on the wisdom of past ages when wrestling with the difficult parts of Scripture. We should look especially to the writers of the Early Church and others who strove after holiness above all and embraced the spirit of primitive Christianity. Because of our openness to learning from the Christians of past ages, we reject the view of biblicists that only the Bible should be used to interpret the Bible, as well as the view of modernists that the findings of recent scholarship are the only acceptable source of guidance for understanding the Scriptures. Wesleyan interpretation lies closer to the views of traditionalists, who insist that the Bible must be interpreted in harmony with those authors whom the tradition of the church has declared orthodox. Unlike the traditionalists, however, Wesleyan Christians place the greatest emphasis on holiness and the ethos of primitive Christianity, and thus we do not confine ourselves to those authors whom councils, popes, synods, and confessions have decreed to be orthodox. In our struggle with the hard parts of Scripture we truly are surrounded by a great "cloud of witnesses."

Understanding God's Mercy and Wrath with the Early Church

So how does a Wesleyan-traditionalist approach help us with those verses from Exodus 34 mentioned above? In the remainder of this chapter, I would like to model how authors from the Early Church can help us understand a difficult passage of Scripture such as that. Because there was a great deal of debate over God's justice and mercy in the early centuries of Christianity, the writings of the Early Church are especially helpful for Wesleyan readers. Then, as now, there were many Christians who insisted that the OT and the NT portrayed different gods. In this next part of the chapter, we will examine some of these views and then turn to how two of the Fathers of the Church, Origen of Alexandria and Ephrem the Syrian, answered the challenge of difficult texts like Exodus 34:6-7.

The Heretics

In the early centuries of Christianity, many groups believed that the OT and the NT spoke of two different gods. Although on the surface level this appears similar to popular ideas today, there are actually some important differences. People today who see different portrayals of God in the Old and New Testaments tend to see the teaching of Jesus as superseding those of the OT. In this view, the OT is old and out of date, immature in comparison with the NT. In other words, the NT replaces the OT. In contrast, those in the early centuries of Christianity who saw different gods in the two testaments did not tell a story of historical development, in which humanity moved from a primitive and barbaric picture to a more enlightened one. Rather, these heretical groups, such as the Gnostics, Valentinians, and Marcionites, saw in the different gods they perceived in the Old and New Testaments two distinct and opposed spiritual powers.

Although these heretical groups all agreed that the God described in the OT, the one who created the cosmos and gave the Law to Israel, was different from the God described in the NT, who sent his Son Jesus to bring salvation to the world, they differed greatly among themselves on other points. Some of these heretics believed that the God of the OT was a malevolent and ignorant being, who did not realize that he was not the supreme being of the universe. Heretics who shared this belief, often referred to as the Gnostics, wrote expanded versions of the stories of Genesis, such as *The Hypostasis of the Archons* and *The Apocryphon of John*, which developed their interpretation of the text and portrayed the God of the OT as a wicked demon. Other heretics, such as the Valentinian teacher Ptolemy, held that the God who gave the Law to Israel could not have been wholly evil, since there were some good laws, but neither could he be the perfectly good God of the NT, since there were other laws that were less than perfect. Meanwhile, the Marcionites held that the God of the NT, the Father of Jesus Christ, is perfectly good and loving, extending his grace to all, while the God of the OT is perfectly, ruthlessly just, meting out punishment with no room for forgiveness.

There is a common misconception that these heretical groups did not consider the OT to be Scripture. Although the Gnostics, Valentinians, and Marcionites did not consider the God described in the OT to be the same as the God of the NT, the Father of Jesus, they all nevertheless considered the writings of the OT to be sources for religious knowledge. If they had not considered the writings of the OT important, they would not have spent so much time interpreting them. The Gnostics, as I already mentioned, wrote elaborate expansions of the opening chapters of Genesis to bring out what they considered the true story behind the biblical account. Similarly, Marcion, the founder of the Marcionites, wrote a book called *Antitheses*, in which he catalogued all the contradictions between the OT and the NT, in accord with his idea that Jesus had come to deliver us from the relentlessly, mercilessly just God of Israel. All these heretical groups considered the story of the OT important for understanding Jesus's work and teaching: it told the story of the power he had come to overthrow and the tyranny from which he offered salvation.

Although the beliefs of these heretical groups fall far outside the bounds of orthodox Christianity, they can still be helpful to us today as we struggle with verses like Exodus 34:6-7 and the difficult question of God's mercy and wrath. Knowledge of this history helps us put popular beliefs in our own world about the wrathful "Old Testament God" into a broader context. Learning about this history helps us realize that contemporary Christians are not the first ones to have seen contrast or even contradiction between different portrayals of God in the Bible. These views have not come about in our day because of some special modern insight or perceptive scholarly study: they have always been there as one tempting way to read the Bible.

Studying these ancient heretical views can also point out the incomplete quality of similar contemporary ideas. Gnostic, Valentinian, and Marcionite theologians had really thought through what it would mean for Christian belief if the OT was truly depicting a God different from the Father of Jesus. Because Jesus himself, as well as the authors of the NT, make many references to we now call the OT, the heretics could not just ignore and discard it completely. Instead, they reasoned out complex theological systems. By contrast, modern ideas about the "Old Testament God" lack the depth and rigor of these heretical interpretations and tend to fall back on the idea that all of revelation, New Testament as well as Old, is merely a collection of human reflections.

Origen of Alexandria

Although these heretical ideas from the ancient church shed some light on contemporary responses to verses like Exodus 34:6-7, they do not actually move us much closer to understanding the verses themselves. For that we can turn to those Christians who argued against the theology of the Gnostics, Valentinians, and Marcionites. One of the most prominent and enduring voices from among these orthodox Christians was a man named Origen of Alexandria. Born in 184 CE in Alexandria, Egypt, Origen grew up in a time when Christianity was subject to sporadic persecution in the Roman Empire. Origen experienced this persecution firsthand when he was still a teenager; his father Leonides was martyred for his faith. After his father's death, Origen supported his family by becoming a teacher. Soon he was renowned throughout the church as a theologian and, above all, as an interpreter of Scripture.

Origen was one of the first Christians to write commentaries on books of the Bible and either preached through or wrote a commentary on nearly every book of Scripture. He also wrote works defending Christianity against the critiques of pagans and a work called *On First Principles*, which offered an outline of Christian belief and is considered by many to be the first work of systematic theology. At the end of his life, when Christians in the Roman Empire faced the first empire-wide persecution under the Emperor Decius, Origen, as a prominent teacher of the Church, was imprisoned and tortured. He died less than a year later as a result of the wounds he had suffered.

Although he dedicated his life's work to uncovering the full meaning of the Bible, Origen was also eager to show the insufficiency and error of heretical interpretations of Scripture. Chief among these was the idea that the OT and the NT depicted different Gods. In *On First Principles*, Origen dedicated a whole section to correcting this heretical view (*Princ.* 2.4-5). He pointed out many passages in the NT (e.g. Matt. 22:34-40) that show Jesus's approval of the OT Law and others (such as Stephen's speech in Acts 7) that clearly show that the God described in the OT is the same as the One who raised Jesus from the dead and sent the Holy Spirit. He also notes that God is described as being wrathful not only in the Old Testament, but in the NT as well, especially in parables (e.g., Luke 19:12-27).

For our purposes, the most important aspect of Origen's argument is his contention that God can be both good and just. Origen points out that, in order to say that the one God cannot be both good and just, the heretics have to have a very cramped understanding of goodness and justice (*Princ.* 2.5.1). The heretics seem to think that in order to be good, God must only ever do things that are obviously beneficial and could never do things that we experience as harsh or painful. On the other hand, the heretics seem to hold that if God were just and punished the wicked, it would necessarily mean that God hated them and intended, somewhat sadistically, only to do them harm by punishing them. However, Origen argues, if we do not hold to these cramped concepts of justice and goodness, it is quite easy to see how God can be both good and just, both slow to anger and visiting punishment, as described in Exodus 34. If God were both good and just it would mean that divine punishments, even if painful, are not meant sadistically to do harm, but rather are given for the benefit of those who suffer them.

Now, that can appear somewhat counter intuitive in the abstract. Elsewhere in his works, however, Origen often gives two concrete examples to illustrate what he means. The first example is medicine. It is not for nothing that we talk about "having to take your medicine." Things that benefit us greatly can often be very unpleasant to experience. This is especially true when we think of something like surgery, where doctors literally cut open a body (something that would normally be considered harmful and violent) in order to repair it. The second example Origen often turns to comes from human relationships, especially child rearing. When a parent disciplines or corrects a child, they are doing it for the child's ultimate benefit, even if it is painful or upsetting for the child in the moment. Often the child is upset with being disciplined because they may not understand why they should not be allowed to hit people or take their toys, but such discipline will ultimately help them to grow into an adult. The parent can be both just and good when disciplining their child (*Homilies on Jeremiah* 20.3).

So how can Origen's concept of God being both just and good help us to understand Exodus 34:6-7? Let's look back at some of the details of the text, as Origen always would when he was interpreting the Bible. One thing Origen might notice is that in the first part of this text, where God is good and merciful, we find adjectives that describe *who God is*: "a God merciful and gracious, slow to anger, and abounding in steadfast love and faithfulness." In the second part, by contrast, where God is being just, God only describes *actions*: "by no means clearing the guilty, but visiting the iniquity of the parents upon the children and the children's children." God does not say, "I am merciful and gracious—but I am also violent and cruel." What God says is "I am merciful and gracious, even though one of my acts, as a merciful and gracious God, is to punish the wicked." This must mean, Origen would tell us, that when God punishes, it has not changed who God is: God is still merciful and gracious. In this way, God is both good and just.

As we continue to look at the details of these verses, is there any indication of Origen's idea that God's punishment is ultimately for our benefit? This detail is a little subtler. Look back at these verses and notice how long God's steadfast love endures, and compare it with how long the punishments endure. God "keeps steadfast love for the thousandth generation, forgiving iniquity and transgression and sin," but "visits the iniquity of the parents upon the children and the children's children to the third and fourth generation." The punishment for sin lasts for three or four generations, but the steadfast love of God lasts for a thousand! That is quite a contrast. In fact, the contrast is even greater than that. As I mentioned above, in biblical idiom "the thousandth generation" should be taken to mean effectively forever. Since Origen always encourages his readers to remember that not everything in the Bible is meant to be taken exactly literally, he would almost certainly agree with this interpretation. The punishment of sin lasts for three or four generations, but the steadfast love of God lasts *forever*. The period of punishment is vanishingly brief by comparison with the period of steadfast love. The ten minutes a child spends in time-out is similarly brief in comparison with the lifetime of their parents' love. From this contrast we might infer with Origen that divine punishments ultimately serve the purposes of God's steadfast love. God's justice *is* good.

This idea that God is both good and just had major implications for Origen's theology. Origen was convinced from his reading of Scripture that all beings would be saved and eventually inherit eternal bliss. If God's punishments are ultimately for our good, why would the punishments of hell be any different? According to Origen, as we have seen, God never punishes someone simply to punish them, but always as part of a plan to bring them to salvation. Origen thus considered even the punishments of hell to be part of God's plan to correct our iniquities and purify us of our sins. Because God desires us to become truly good, perfectly holy as God is holy, the divine plan of salvation intends to actually transform us. The course of treatment might prove long and painful, but a rich and healthy life ultimately lies on the other side of it—and we could not get to that full life without moving through the difficult period of therapy. The three or four generations of punishment will ultimately lead to the thousand generations of steadfast love.

Because of his belief in universal salvation—as well as some other teachings and a healthy dose of ugly Early Church politics—in 543, Emperor Justinian I condemned him as a heretic and ordered all his writings to be burned. Yet, many consider Origen as one of the greatest teachers the church ever produced. Nevertheless, even those Wesleyans who subscribe to the belief that there will be some who are eternally damned can still draw on Origen's profound insights when wrestling with the difficult parts of Scripture. Origen, just like John Wesley's favorite figures from the Early Church, exhibited the spirit of "primitive Christianity" in his earnest and continual striving after holiness, seen most clearly his refusal to give in to the enticements of worldly prestige, which led him to endure torture during the Decian persecution and eventually die as a result of the wounds he suffered for Christ. Whether we agree with all his ideas or not, Origen always proves a valuable resource for our struggles with the hard parts of Scripture.

Ephrem the Syrian

In the generations after Origen's death a great deal changed for the Christians of the Roman Empire. The empire-wide persecutions that had begun under the Emperor Decius continued under some of his successors, culminating in the "Great Persecution" under the Emperor Diocletian. Then, when all seemed darkest, their fortunes took a sudden turn for the better under the Emperor Constantine, who proclaimed religious toleration throughout the Empire, lavishly patronized the church, and was even baptized on his deathbed. Ephrem the Syrian belonged to this first generation of Christians to come of age in the post-persecution world of Constantine and his successors.

Ephrem was born and lived most of his life in the city of Nisibis (modern Nusaybin, Turkey). In Ephrem's day, this proud Mesopotamian city sat on the contested frontier between the Roman Empire and the Sasanian Persian Empire or Eranshahr. Nisibis was under constant threat of warfare throughout Ephrem's life as successive Roman emperors and the Sasanian Shahanshah Shapur the Great struggled for mastery. Despite the failure of several Sasanian sieges of Nisibis, the city was eventually surrendered to Shapur the Great in 363 CE. A condition of the surrender was that all the Christians would leave the city, forcing Ephrem and his entire community to become refugees. Thus, although by Ephrem's time the age of persecution in the Roman Empire, which so marked Origen's life had ended, Ephrem nevertheless endured the traumas of war and exile. Ephrem spent the last ten years of his life in the city of Edessa, where we are told that he eventually died while tending to the sick during an outbreak of the plague.

Despite the turmoil that marked his life, Ephrem, like Origen, was an incredibly prolific author. Ephrem wrote in the Syriac language, a dialect of Aramaic, producing commentaries on many of the books of the Bible as well as treatises refuting the beliefs of the heretics. He is most famous, however, for his poems and hymns, which have earned him the title "The Harp of the Spirit." These poems are divided mainly into two genres: *madrashe*, which are didactic lyric poems, and *memre*, which are sermons in verse. Ephrem's ancient biographers tell us that many of his *madrashe* were written to be performed by a women's choir, which he also directed; some of his *memre* may well have been composed extemporaneously. In his verse, Ephrem mixes the sublimity of poetic art with subtle theological argumentation and profound biblical exegesis. Although some Christian traditions would be hesitant to draw on a poet for insights into theology and scriptural interpretation, we Wesleyan Christians, formed by the hymns of Charles Wesley and others, recognize kindred spirits in Ephrem's Syriac church.

Although Ephrem the Syrian (306–373 CE) lived about a hundred years after Origen, many of the same debates about God's justice and goodness still raged in his day. In Ephrem's day the Marcionites in particular remained prominent, while the Valentinians and Gnostics had begun to fade away, especially in Ephrem's part of the world. As Ephrem composed his commentaries, treatises, and poems, he was always vigilant to correct the prevalent Marcionite idea that separated the God of the OT from the God of the New (Lieu 2015, 151–176). Ephrem was particularly passionate in arguing against the idea that the true God, the Father of Jesus, did not create this material world. Ephrem playfully reminded the Marcionites that they themselves valued things like food, water, and shelter, all of them gifts of the one who sustains the material world—if they call these things good, how could they say the God who provides them is not good, but only just? Ephrem was also fond of pointing out how much time Jesus spent in healing physical ailments. Why would he heal the sick and the broken if he did not think the material world and its creatures were good? (*Against Marcion*, C. W. Mitchell 2008).

Like Origen, Ephrem also emphasized that God could be both gracious and just. According to Ephrem, God prefers to be gracious, allowing human beings to work things out through their own free will instead of coercing them through chastisement and discipline. Nevertheless, because God desires what is good for his creatures, he will also punish the wicked, both in order to correct them and to serve as a warning to others. However, even there, God's grace is preeminent. God is always eager to seize on even the briefest moment of repentance as an excuse to stay his wrath and treat sinful human beings far more leniently than they deserve. Thus, although Ephrem teaches that God is both gracious and just, his grace and generosity take precedence over his justice. In his poems, Ephrem writes exuberantly about how God delights to shower humanity with blessings far in excess of what we deserve.

Although Ephrem and Origen agree on the basic principle that God is both good and just, Ephrem's answer to the Marcionites has a different emphasis than his predecessor's. Origen argued that God could be good in a way that was just and just in a way that was good, as in the example of a parent who disciplines a child. Instead of teaching that God's goodness is just, and God's justice good, Ephrem emphasizes that, although God can be just, God is gracious above all. God is always looking for reasons to be gracious and merciful, even when our sinful behavior gives no reason for it. In the second *madrasha* of his *Hymns on Nisibis*, Ephrem even compares God to a clever lawyer who does some "creative accounting" with humanity's debts so as to have an excuse for being merciful (*Hymns on Nisibis* 2.12–14). Likewise, although at the Last Judgment God's justice must deliver punishment and reward according to each person's deeds, Ephrem preaches that even the least repentance becomes a pretext for God to tip the scales in favor of grace.

Because God is gracious above all, divine punishment is for the benefit of God's creatures. Ephrem expresses this eloquently through a reflection on the examples of Jesus casting out the demon Legion (Mark 5:1-20) and his cursing of the fig tree (Mark 11:12-14):

> Not with menacing threat did he rebuke and save:
> Though he declares "Woe!" his nature is to make peace,
> And though he rebukes the devil he is entirely calm.
> Not from wrath did he command the swine
> To cast themselves into the sea, nor was it out of hatred he shriveled
> The fig with his imprecations, for in all he does he is good.
> —*Hymns on Paradise* 12.14

So how can Ephrem's ideas about God's grace and justice help us to understand Exodus 34:6-7? As we did with Origen, let us look at the details of the passage. Once again, notice how the divine self-descriptions begin with the claim that God is gracious and merciful and spend more time describing God's mercy and love than the punishments that God visits on the wicked. In the descriptions about punishing the wicked, God does not give it equal time or equal prominence. Ephrem might say that this should remind us that God is above all merciful—not a wrathful, bullying God who is occasionally merciful nor a God who is equally punitive and forgiving. God is entirely gracious and good, and when God punishes, it is always subordinated to that goodness. "Though he declares 'Woe!' his nature is to make peace."

Conclusion

So, where does this leave us with a difficult passage like Exodus 34:6-7? Hopefully these insights from Origen and Ephrem (and even the heretics) have helped to make sense of a God, who both forgives and punishes and is still good and merciful. This does not mean that they necessarily have tied it all up in a neat bow: the Fathers of the Church are not "the answers in the back of the book." As Wesleyan Christians we seek out the wisdom of those who have gone before us in the faith, and we are eager to learn from exemplars of the spirit of primitive Christianity like Origen and Ephrem. Nevertheless, we do not look to our fellow believers from other ages as unquestionable authorities. Because they have made the journey before us, we view them as trustworthy guides, but that does not mean they know the only path to travel.

For Wesleyans, any drawing on the treasury of the Christian past is governed by our yearning to be, like John Wesley, "people of one book," committing ourselves to the Scriptures in our quest for holiness of heart and life. In that sense, although we value immensely the testimony and teaching of our forebears in the faith, as well as the guidance of acceptable orthodoxy and the insights of scholarly inquiry, none of that can replace our own personal encounter with Jesus the Living Word in the words of the Bible. To come to an understanding of passages like Exodus 34:6-7, we must spend time above all with Scripture itself, as well as with the other means of grace, such as prayer, and we must live out the commandments of love in our actions. With the Living Word we must do that wrestling that Jacob did at Peniel (Gen. 32:2-32). We must not be afraid to work at it, just as we Wesleyans strive to "work on your own salvation with fear and trembling" (Phil. 2:12).

In his *Commentary on the Psalms,* Origen used a parable he learned from one of his teachers to explain this work of scriptural interpretation, which is at the same time the work of sanctification, that most Wesleyan of ends. He said that Scripture is like a vast palace containing innumerable rooms. As we wander this mysterious palace, we find that each of the rooms is locked. In front of each of these locked doors we find a key, but it is a key to another door. The task of interpreting Scripture is to match the keys we find at one door to the locks they actually open (*Philocalia* 2.3). Perhaps ancient authors like Origen and Ephrem can help you match the keys you have picked up in your journey with Scripture to the doors that have been shut to you, opening up the treasures of grace within. And perhaps you have the key to a door that even they could not unlock.

References

Campbell, Ted. 1991. *John Wesley and Christian Antiquity: Religious Vision and Cultural Change*. Nashville: Abingdon Press.

Ephrem the Syrian. 1990. *Hymns on Paradise*. Translated by Sebastian Brock. Crestwood, NY: St. Vladimir's Seminary Press.

Lieu, Judith. 2015. *Marcion and the Making of a Heretic: God and Scripture in the Second Century*. Cambridge: Cambridge University Press.

Maddox, Randy. 2012. "John Wesley— 'A Man of One Book.'" In *Wesley, Wesleyans, and Reading Bible as Scripture*, edited by Joel Green and David Watson, 3–18. Waco: Baylor University Press, 2012.

Mitchell, C. W. 1912–1921. *S. Ephraim's Prose Refutations of Mani, Marcion, and Bardaisan*. Completed by A.A. Bevan and F.C. Burkitt. 2 vols. London: Williams and Norgate.

Origen of Alexandria. 2019. *On First Principles (A Reader's Edition)*. Translated by John Behr. Oxford: Oxford University Press.

———. 1998. *Homilies on Jeremiah and 1 Kings 28*. Translated by John Clark Smith. Washington, D.C.: The Catholic University of America Press.

———. 2024. *The Philocalia of Origen: A New Translation with Annotations*. Translated by Ronald Heine. Oxford: Oxford University Press.

Ephrem of Nisibis. 1898. *Hymns on Nisibis*. Translated by J.T. Stopford in *Nicene and Post-Nicene Fathers*, Second Series, Volume XIII, Part II. Oxford: Hendrickson.

Wesley, John. "On God's Vineyard," (Sermon 107). Wesley Center Online. http://wesley.nnu.edu/john-wesley/the-sermons-of-john-wesley-1872-edition/sermon-107-on-gods-vineyard/.

———. "The Wisdom of God's Counsels," (Sermon 68). Wesley Center Online. http://wesley.nnu.edu/john-wesley/the-sermons-of-john-wesley-1872-edition/sermon-68-the-wisdom-of-gods-counsels/.

For Further Reading

Brock, Sebastian. 1992. *The Luminous Eye: The Spiritual World Vision of Saint Ephrem the Syrian*. Kalamazoo, MI: Cistercian Publications.

Heine, Ronald. 2012. *Origen: Scholarship in the Service of the Church*. Oxford: Oxford University Press.

CHAPTER 6

'A Conviction of Insufficiency'

John Wesley's Approach to Old Testament Scholarship

Diana Abernethy

Late in his life and much to his surprise, John Wesley found himself writing his *Explanatory Notes Upon the Old Testament*. His *Explanatory Notes Upon the New Testament* had been so appreciated in the Methodist movement that he was encouraged to produce a similar resource on the Old Testament (OT). Although he was a bit daunted by the challenges the project would present, he devised a way to equip Methodists who sought to dive deeper in their study of the OT. For his *Explanatory Notes Upon the Old Testament*, Wesley wrote a Preface containing fascinating insights into his thinking about biblical interpretation.

In this Preface, Wesley explains his motivations, his processes, and his hopes for his notes. Though he acknowledges the challenges of writing them, he describes why he perseveres. In his descriptions, readers glimpse why Wesley understands these notes to be worth his efforts. He recognized he needed to supplement his limited study of the OT, and he appreciated how much time these notes would take in a season of life when so many tasks called for his attention. Wesley was compelled to complete this project by his deep conviction that "searching the Scriptures" is a means of grace, in which Christians receive God's love and guidance. He pressed on because he believed such encounters with God are a generous gift from God and a vital part of the Christian life.

As Wesley explains his process, he describes how he found a way forward in spite of his lack of in-depth study of the OT. He decides to abridge commentaries by faithful and respected biblical scholars, and he details why he selected the work of Matthew Henry and Matthew Poole, as well as how he drew on their work. Wesley also reveals some of his goals for his *Explanatory Notes Upon the Old Testament:* he wants these notes to be a practical resource for Methodists with a wide range of educational backgrounds, and his concern for accessibility shapes the kind of notes he crafts. Additionally, Wesley stresses that his notes should be "spiritual" in the sense that they guide Christians in their discipleship. This concern informs his selection of what resources to use and how to use them.

Below, I explore four insights into Wesleyan biblical interpretation that arise from Wesley's explanations of his motivations, process, and goals in his Preface to the *Explanatory Notes Upon the Old Testament*:

1) "Searching the Scriptures" is a means of grace.
2) Biblical scholarship can be a vibrant gift for Christians.
3) Christians benefit from having accessible resources for biblical interpretation.
4) Such resources should contribute to growth in Christian discipleship.

After illuminating how these insights arise in Wesley's explanations in the Preface, this chapter examines Wesley's notes on Numbers 21:4-9 to show how Wesley incorporated these insights into his notes. In conclusion, this is a discussion how the observations from Wesley's Preface to his *Explanatory Notes Upon the Old Testament* can inform how Wesleyans practice and interpret the Bible.

"Searching the Scriptures" as a Means of Grace

For Wesley, "searching the Scriptures" is a means of grace, and he alludes to this at the end of the Preface. Yet, he describes the concept in greater detail in his sermon, "The Means of Grace" (Sermon 16). In it, he explains that the means of grace are "outward signs, words, or actions, ordained by God, and appointed for this end, to be the ordinary channels whereby he might convey to men preventing, justifying, or sanctifying grace" (II.1). That is, God intends God's people to engage in certain practices regularly, and through these practices, God will meet them, and they will receive grace. Although God is free to meet them in other places as well, these practices provide contexts in which people can expect to meet God. These means of grace thus guide God's people in what to do to grow closer to God and to become more faithful disciples of Christ.

Wesley names several means of grace that form the foundation of the Christian life. After prayer, he identifies "searching the Scriptures" as the second principal means of grace ("The Means of Grace," II.1). He explains how he derives his list from precedents in the NT. Jesus himself commends "searching the Scriptures" because they "testify" to Jesus and lead people to believe in Him (John 5:39). Acts 17:11-12 provides an example of people studying the Scriptures and coming to faith in Jesus. Wesley also cites 2 Timothy 3:15-17 to recommend searching the Scriptures as a path to growth in wisdom and discipleship. He recognizes that the "Scriptures" to which 2 Timothy refers are "primarily" from what is now known as the OT, since the NT had not yet been written. Wesley reflects this insight in practice when he reads from the OT and NT in his daily devotions and encourages Methodists to do likewise (Preface, 18). From Jesus's command and the teaching of the apostles, Wesley advocates "searching the Scriptures" as a primary way Christians grow in their understanding and love of God ("The Means of Grace," III.7).

In this sermon, Wesley specifies that "searching the Scriptures" involves "reading, hearing, and meditating" on the Scriptures. Therefore, he encourages Methodists to open themselves to God by reading, as well as hearing, the Scriptures. Since Wesley includes both reading and hearing, a range of contexts can be opportunities to practice this means of grace—including hearing the Scriptures during worship services, reading them during personal devotions, hearing the Scriptures during small group and family devotions, and many others. These practices are only the first step, because Wesley also encourages Christians to consider Scripture deeply by meditating on it.

Meditating on Scripture includes careful study, thoughtful reflection, and exploring the many details of the texts. Individuals can meditate on Scripture in their own devotions, and small groups, holy friends, and families can converse about their observations to see more in the texts. Because "searching the Scriptures" entails meditating on it, guides like Wesley's *Explanatory Notes Upon the Old Testament* can help Christians with their deeper explorations of Scripture.

When Wesley concludes the Preface, section 17, of his *Explanatory Notes Upon the Old Testament*, he emphasizes the need to meditate on the Scriptures, and his appeal draws on his understanding of searching the Scriptures as a means of grace. He writes:

> This is the way to understand the things of God; Meditate thereon day and night; So shall you attain the best knowledge; even to know the only true God and Jesus Christ whom He hath sent. And this knowledge will lead you, to love Him, because he hath first loved us: yea, to love the Lord your God with all your heart, and with all your soul, and with all your mind, and with all your strength. Will there not then be all that mind in you, which was also in Christ Jesus[?] And in consequence of this, while you joyfully experience all the holy tempers described in this book, you will likewise be outwardly holy as He that hath called you is holy, in all manner of conversation (Wesley 1975, 1:ix).

Wesley explains that this careful consideration of Scripture leads Christians to deeper knowledge of God and of Jesus. However, this knowledge is not the only goal. Knowledge of God leads to love of God. Wesley sees this call to love as a central theme running through Scripture.[1] Here, he alludes to Matthew 22:36-40 (see also Mark 12:28-31; Luke 10:26-28) where Jesus quotes Deuteronomy the greatest commandment: "You shall love the LORD your God with all of your heart and with all of your soul and with all of your might" (Deut. 6:5). By including "with all your mind," Wesley rightly clarifies that this call to love includes loving God with one's thoughts, which is implied in the Hebrew words used in Deuteronomy 6:5. He connects the call to love God with one's entire mind with the command in Philippians 2:1-5

---

1. For more on this theme in Wesley's work, see Maddox, Randy 2011. "The Rule of Christian Faith, Practice, and Hope: John Wesley on the Bible," *Methodist Review* 3:1-35.

to have "the same mind" as that of Jesus. As knowledge of God leads to love of God, it transforms the Christian. The Christian then becomes "outwardly holy" and is guided by "holy tempers"—inner dispositions working within them. For Wesley, knowledge and love of God play a central role in sanctification, in which the Holy Spirit guides Christians to put their love into action by living as faithful disciples. In sum, Wesley views searching the Scriptures as vital because it inspires the knowledge and love of God that transform the lives of Christians.

At the end of the Preface, Wesley clarifies his main motivation for producing his *Explanatory Notes Upon the Old Testament*: because searching the Scriptures is a means of grace, it has the power to transform Christians into more faithful disciples. This deep conviction drove him to write these notes, even when he felt tired and inadequate to the task. At the beginning of the Preface in section 2, he expresses great surprise that he finds himself undertaking such demanding work at his advanced age: "And to this day it appears to me as a dream, a thing almost incredible, that I should be entering upon a work of this kind, when I am entering into the sixty-third year of my age" (Wesley 1975, 1:iii). Yet, despite the challenges, Wesley persevered, compelled by his desire to equip Methodists to grow in knowledge of God, love of God, and holiness.

Fruits of Biblical Scholarship

While the benefits of searching the Scriptures drive Wesley, he also confesses his reluctance to produce such a guide. His reluctance reflects his appreciation of in-depth biblical scholarship. Wesley names two specific reasons for his hesitancy. He laments his lack of time, particularly since it would take a significant amount of time to produce his own detailed study of the OT. In section 2 of the Preface, he additionally recognizes his inadequacy to produce a suitable resource on his own:

> Over and above the deep conviction I had, of my insufficiency for such a work, of my want of learning, of understanding, of spiritual experience, for an undertaking more difficult by many degrees, than even writing on the New Testament, I objected, that there were many passages in the Old, which I did not understand myself, and consequently could not explain to others, either to their satisfaction, or my own (Wesley 1975: 1:iii).

Wesley confesses that he struggles to understand parts of the OT, and this concerns him as he prepares to write his notes on the OT. He also specifies some reasons that contribute to those struggles. When he notes his lack of "spiritual experience," he reveals his conviction that one's piety and maturity as a disciple contribute to one's ability to understand Scripture. Wesley also identifies his lack of "learning"—although he studied at Oxford on his way to ordination, he recognizes that others have studied the OT more deeply than he has. He perceives how in-depth study of the OT by some can yield insights that aid many Christians as they search the Scriptures. As Wesley recognizes the limits of his study, he conveys both respect for detailed biblical scholarship and a conviction that such studies can be beneficial for Christians who are growing as faithful disciples.

Wesley's concerns about his inadequate knowledge led him to conclude that he could not produce notes on the OT on his own, but he found another way to proceed. He decided to work from existing Bible commentaries to produce more condensed notes on the OT that are specifically tailored to Christians with a wide range of educational backgrounds. To craft this practical resource, Wesley began with the work of well-respected biblical commentators of his time, and then he abridged it. He selected two commentaries for his main references—Matthew Henry's *Exposition of the Old and New Testaments* and Matthew Poole's *English Annotations on the Holy Bible*.

Wesley explains that he selected Matthew Henry's commentary as his starting point because of Henry's understanding and faithfulness: "He is allowed by all competent judges," writes Wesley in section 3 of the Preface, "to have been a person of strong understanding, of various learning, of solid piety, and much experience in the ways of God" (Wesley 1975, 1:iii). Because Henry has extensively studied the Scriptures, he is able to write an informed and thorough commentary, and Henry's personal piety and mature faith guide him to recognize insights in Scripture that inform Christian discipleship. As Wesley recognizes the contributions of both Henry's education and piety, he communicates how important both study and piety are for biblical scholarship that benefits Christians' understanding of the Scriptures.

Later in section 13 of the Preface, Wesley describes his process of drawing on Henry and Poole's work in more detail. First, Wesley clarifies his method when working from Henry's commentary. Wesley presents his own work as far from a "bare abridgement of Mr. Henry's exposition" (Wesley 1975, 1:vii). Although one of Wesley's main goals was to condense Henry's lengthy discussions, Wesley also adds his own insights and shapes Henry's work for a wider audience. Wesley says Henry's goal was "to say as much, whereas it is mine to say as little as possible," and Wesley estimates that he omits "nineteen parts out of twenty" from Henry's commentary (Wesley 1975, 1:vii).

In addition to condensing, Wesley makes Henry's writing more accessible in several ways. Wesley discusses some stylistic changes that he makes to Henry's comments, including shortening sentences and using more common words in place of more obscure ones. As Wesley changes Henry's phrasing to make it "more clear and determinate," he admits his caution not to change the meaning of Henry's points too much. Wesley is reluctant to make significant changes, as he writes in section 14, because he is "conscious of [his own] very imperfect acquaintance with the Hebrew tongue" (Wesley 1975, 1:vii). Wesley's caution here illustrates another dimension of his respect for biblical scholarship. Because Hebrew is the original language of most of the OT, Henry's command of Hebrew allows him to see aspects of the OT that can be harder to recognize in translation. Wesley appreciates how knowledge of Hebrew contributes to biblical scholarship that is a gift to Christians who search the Scriptures.

While Wesley appreciates Henry's work for the ways it grows out of his knowledge of Hebrew, extensive study, and piety, Wesley also recognizes shortcomings in Henry's work for Wesley's goal of producing notes that are accessible to a wide range of Christians. Wesley observes that Henry does not always explain terms and phrases in Scripture because he assumed his readers would be familiar with them and did not want to repeat the work of other commentators (Preface, 10). Wesley identifies this as a key shortcoming for his goal of producing a resource that will be accessible to a wide range of Christians. To remedy this lack, Wesley draws on Matthew Poole's *English Annotations on the Holy Bible* because Henry himself praises Poole's work and expresses his intention to avoid repeating Poole's observations. Although Henry encourages his readers to consult Poole's work in addition to his own, Wesley recognizes that many of his readers will not have access to either Henry's or Poole's volumes, much less those of both. To craft his accessible resource, Wesley decides to draw on the work of both Henry and Poole to give his readers the benefit of both of their insights in one place.

Wesley explains how he incorporated insights from Henry's and Poole's commentaries. In section 14 Wesley indicates that he initially planned to consult Henry's work and then supplement what he drew from it with additional explanations from Poole's work. However, after Wesley worked through Genesis in preparing his notes, he adjusted his method. He shifted his process so that he first consulted Poole's commentary and then supplemented Poole's insights with those from Henry. Wesley selected sections of Henry's work that helpfully added to Poole's observations. Wesley emphasizes that he not only incorporated many insights from Poole and Henry in his *Explanatory Notes Upon the Old Testament* but that he also added his own contributions to make his notes better serve his goals.

When Wesley explains his process of drawing on Henry's and Poole's commentaries in detail, his dependence on their work is clear. This dependence is a testament to Wesley's conviction that in-depth studies of Scripture, like those of Henry and Poole, can yield insights that aid Christians searching the Scriptures. Although Wesley deeply appreciates their work, his adaptations of their commentaries illustrate some of Wesley's specific goals for his *Explanatory Notes Upon the Old Testament*. His explanations of his method reveal his intention to produce a resource that is accessible to Christians with a wider range of educational backgrounds and that significantly contributes to their growth in discipleship.

Fruits of Accessible Resources

As Wesley describes how he draws on the work of Henry and Poole, it is clear that Wesley intends to produce a guide that is practical for Christians with a wide range of educational backgrounds. Since studying the Scriptures is such a vital means of grace, Wesley seeks to assist many Christians in this practice. He explains how he made his notes more accessible than Henry's commentary in three principal ways: Wesley's notes will be more affordable, shorter, and written in simpler language.

Although Wesley praises the virtues of Henry's commentary, he explains its practical limitations for many Christians. Wesley first raises concerns about the cost of Henry's commentary and notes that it would be quite unaffordable for many working-class Methodists of his time. He also recognizes that the length of the commentary would present challenges for those Methodists who had limited time for leisure and reading. In response to these practical concerns, Wesley endeavored to make his notes both shorter and more affordable so that they would be more accessible to working-class Methodists of his day.

In addition to cost and length, Wesley also aims to use language that is more accessible to Methodists with a wide range of educational backgrounds. He discusses his goal to make his notes "plainer as well as shorter" in section 8 of the Preface (Wesley 1975, 1:v). As he writes in a more accessible way, Wesley draws on his pastoral experiences of conversing with diverse audiences. Continuing section 8 of the Preface, he argues that these experiences are essential for knowing how to communicate effectively with those who would find the language of Henry's commentary inaccessible:

> It is not by reading, much less by musing alone, that we are enabled to suit our discourse to common capacities. It is only by actually talking with the vulgar, that we learn to talk in a manner they can understand. And unless we do this, what do we profit them[?] Do we not lose all our labour[?] Should we speak as angels, we should be of no more use to them, than sounding brass or a tinkling cymbal (Wesley 1975, 1:v).

While Wesley acknowledges Henry's eloquence, he echoes Paul in 1 Corinthians 13:1 as he contends that failing to communicate in effective language is a failure of love. Wesley views writing in accessible language as a work of love for his neighbors who lack the education to understand Henry's commentary. For Wesley, this effective communication grows out of relationships: because he actually talks to people with a range of educational backgrounds, he knows how to write in language they will understand. While Wesley appreciates that those with the education, time, and financial resources to access Henry's commentary will find it beneficial, Wesley intends to extend some of these benefits to a much wider audience.

Fruits of Discipleship

Because Wesley believes that searching the Scriptures is a means of grace that can transform Christians into more faithful disciples, he specifically crafts his notes to assist Christians on this journey. When Wesley says he hopes his notes are "spiritual," he describes how they can guide Christians in worshipping God and living as disciples of Christ. Wesley's emphasis on the spiritual dimensions of his notes appears in both his praise of Henry's commentary and in his reflections about how to augment Henry's work.

As Wesley explains why he selected Henry's commentary as one of the sources for his notes, he indicates that the spiritual dimensions of Henry's work were an important factor in his choice. Wesley observes that Henry's commentary is "agreeable to the tenor of Scripture, and to the analogy of faith" (Wesley 1975, 1:iii). These phrases highlight central aspects of Wesley's understanding of how Christians should interpret Scripture. Scott Jones explains Wesley's use of these key terms. Wesley refers to the "tenor" of Scripture as the message of Scripture as a whole and how key Christian doctrines constitute this tenor of Scripture (Jones 1995, 43–53). For Wesley, the analogy of faith involves interpreting passages of Scripture in light of these key doctrines, especially Wesley's understanding of the way of salvation. In the way of salvation, humans need God's pardon for sin, which they receive in justification when they have faith in Christ, and the Holy Spirit works in Christians to cultivate holiness in their life, which is seen through their love of God and their neighbors. Therefore, when Wesley praises Henry's commentary for resonating with the tenor of Scripture and the analogy of faith, Wesley recognizes that Henry's interpretations generally agree with understandings of Christian doctrine and the Christian life that Wesley believes will nurture readers in their growth in discipleship.

Wesley also describes Henry's commentary as both practically helpful and "usually spiritual too, teaching us how to worship God, not in form only, but in spirit and in truth" (Wesley 1975, 1:iii). Here, Wesley expresses the importance of guides for helping Christians interpret Scripture and learning how to worship God more faithfully. Wesley specifies that this worship includes not only the outward practices of worship, but also the worship that arises in the heart of a Christian as the Holy Spirit works there to cultivate the love of God and their neighbors. Thus, Wesley's praise of the spiritual dimension of Henry's work reflects Wesley's assessment that Henry's work can guide Christians in their growth in discipleship.

Although Wesley compliments Henry for reflecting on the spiritual dimensions of Scripture, Wesley wishes Henry's commentary had included even more insights connected to discipleship. In section 12, he says Henry's work was "not by any means what I expected" in the sense that he hoped to find more reflections on discipleship (Wesley 1975, 1:vii). For example, Wesley says he had hoped Henry's comments on the Ten Commandments in Exodus 20 would include more connections to Christian practice. Wesley thus planned more reflections on Christian practice in his notes. Immediately after Wesley describes this shortcoming in Henry's commentary in section 12 of the Preface, he explains how he used Henry's work in section 13 of the Preface. This movement from section 12 to 13 implies that one of Wesley's main goals for his notes was to add more reflections on Christian discipleship as he builds on Henry's foundation. Indeed, in section 13, Wesley emphasizes that he not only drew on Henry's work but made "many additions, well nigh from the beginning to the end" (Wesley 1975, 1:vii). By adding more reflection on Christian discipleship in his own notes, Wesley shows how important he believes these reflections are for Christians who are searching the Scriptures.

Wesley also shows his concern for growth in discipleship when he explains his omission of Henry's remarks about "Particular Redemption." Wesley notes that Henry's views on "the doctrine of absolution, irrespective, unconditional Predestination" run throughout his commentary (Wesley 1975, iv.). In his sermon "Free Grace" (Sermon 128), Wesley explains why he rejects the idea of predestination as expressed in the Reformed tradition, which teaches that at the beginning of time, God selected only some people to be saved. Wesley firmly believed that God's love extends to all people, that all people can be justified through faith in Christ, and that they can grow in holiness through the work of the Holy Spirit. For Wesley, Henry's teaching of "Particular Redemption" does not align with key passages in Scripture and can discourage people from striving toward more faithful Christian practice.

Wesley selected Henry's commentary as a source for his notes for its practical and spiritual strengths despite Wesley's disagreement with Henry's views on

"Particular Redemption." Wesley therefore omits Henry's remarks on predestination. For example, Wesley explains in section 9 of the Preface that he does not want to misrepresent Henry's views by changing Henry's phrases, which would give readers the impression that Henry said things he did not. Instead, Wesley simply omits Henry's comments on predestination. Wesley explains:

> Nothing is recited here as written by him which he did not write. Neither is any construction put upon his words, different from his own. But what he wrote in favour of Particular Redemption, is totally left out. And of this I here give express notice to the reader once for all (Wesley 1975, 1:v).

Wesley notifies his readers that he has systematically omitted all of Henry's references to "Particular Redemption," and he gives such notice because he was concerned that those sections could mislead Christians searching the Scriptures. By carefully omitting these sections and adding more reflections on Christian teaching and practice, Wesley shows how important it is for him that his notes provide sound guidance for Christians growing in discipleship.

Reading Scripture with Wesley: Numbers 21:4-9 as a Case Study

After exploring Wesley's explanation of his process and goals in the Preface, readers can see how his aims shaped his *Explanatory Notes Upon the Old Testament*. The idea of searching the Scriptures as a means of grace motivates Wesley to produce these notes, and the notes themselves reflect Wesley's goals. His comments on Numbers 21:4-9 exemplify his convictions that biblical scholarship aids Christians as they search the Scriptures, that his notes should be accessible to working-class Christians, and that his notes should connect to Christian teaching and practice.

In Numbers 21:4-9, the Israelites complain about the manna God has given them during their journey through the wilderness to Canaan, and God sends poisonous snakes as a punishment for their lack of faith. When the people confess their sin, God tells Moses to make a bronze sculpture of a serpent and to hold it up on a pole so that the people can look up at the bronze serpent to be healed. In John 3:14-15, Jesus compares the Son of Man being lifted up to Moses lifting up this bronze serpent. Because of this New Testament reference, Wesley's notes on Numbers 21:4-9 illustrate his emphasis on Christian teaching and practice.

Furthermore, Wesley's notes on Numbers 21:4-9 clearly demonstrate his appreciation of in-depth biblical commentaries. These notes follow those of Poole quite closely, in both phrasing and format. As Wesley explained in section 14 of the Preface, he added "very largely" from Poole's commentary. After Wesley became familiar with both Henry's and Poole's styles and methods by reading their remarks on Genesis, he indicates that he primarily used Poole's observations and supplemented them from Henry's comments at times. Thus, when Wesley follows Poole's comments closely in Numbers 21:4-9, his practice matches his account of his method in the Preface. By drawing so heavily from Poole's commentary in his notes, Wesley demonstrates his appreciation of and reliance on biblical scholarship. By including many of Poole's insights in his notes designed for lay Christians, Wesley shows that he views these insights as beneficial for Christians searching the Scriptures.

In following Poole's format more closely than Henry's, Wesley also illustrates his goal of creating notes that are accessible to working class Christians of his time. In section 13 of the Preface, he characterizes Henry as trying to say as much as possible, while Wesley aims to say as little as possible to convey the main points. Indeed, Henry's notes include much longer expositions on passages of Scripture. In their notes on Numbers 21:4-9, Henry includes 1,927 words, while Wesley includes only 371 words. Wesley's remarks are slightly shorter than Poole's, as Poole includes 418 words on Numbers 21:4-9. As Wesley follows Poole in having much shorter notes than Henry's, Wesley illustrates his intention of making notes that would be practical for Christians with limited time for study.

Wesley also borrows Poole's habit of organizing his remarks around key phrases. Poole often identifies a key phrase from the biblical text and then comments on it, and Wesley retains that format. For example, Wesley's comment on Numbers 21:9 reads, "He lived—He was delivered from death, and cured of his disease." Wesley first identifies the phrase on which he is commenting, here the last phrase in Numbers 21:9, "he lived." Then Wesley includes Poole's explanation of this phrase—each person who looked at the bronze serpent was healed and did not die from their snakebite wounds. The format used by Poole and Wesley is user-friendly because readers can consult the notes when they read a phrase in Scripture that intrigues or puzzles them. Because their remarks often begin with these key phrases, readers can quickly locate their comments on a particular phrase. By following Poole in having shorter notes organized around key phrases, Wesley shows his commitment to producing a more accessible resource than Henry's commentary.

Henry, Poole, and Wesley all comment on the connection between the bronze serpent in Numbers 21:8 and Jesus being lifted on the cross in light of John 3:14-15. In so doing, they show their interest in including Christian teaching in their work. Wesley follows Poole closely in his note on Numbers 21:8, as he only alters a few words from Poole's remarks and thereby endorses Poole's interpretation:

> This method of cure was prescribed, that it might appear to be God's own work, and not the effect of nature or art: and that it might be an eminent type of our salvation by Christ. The serpent signified Christ, who was in the likeness of sinful flesh, though without sin, as this brazen serpent had the outward shape, but not the inward poison, of the other serpents: the pole resembled the cross upon which Christ was lifted up for our salvation: and looking up to it designed our believing in Christ (Wesley 1975, 1:531).

Poole and Wesley draw on earlier traditions of allegorical interpretations of Scripture as they describe the bronze serpent as a "type" of Christ's work. God's work in the Old Testament, as in the bronze serpent, is analogous to what God will do through Christ, and these connections give God's people a preview of what Christ will do for God's people. Thus Poole and Wesley note the similarities between the bronze serpent and Christ in order to show how this Old Testament text contributes to Christian teaching. They focus on two points of comparison. First, the bronze serpent is both similar to and different from the snakes biting the Israelites, which is analogous to how Christ is both similar to and different from other people. The bronze serpent is like the snakes in that they have the same "outward shape," but they differ in that the bronze serpent is not poisonous like the other snakes—the bronze serpent is instead a means by which God will heal the people. Analogously, Christ is human like other people, but unlike other people, Christ did not sin, which is a key part of how Christ's life, death, and resurrection will reconcile people with God. Therefore, the bronze serpent and Christ are similar in that they appear like others but have important differences in relation to their power to heal.

Poole and Wesley also follow John 3:14 in highlighting that both the bronze serpent and Christ are lifted up. In Numbers 21:8-9, God instructs Moses to lift the bronze serpent on a pole so that the Israelites can look up at it and be healed. In John 3:14-15, Jesus explains, "And just as Moses lifted up the serpent in the wilderness, so must the Son of Man be lifted up, that whoever believes in him may have eternal life." For both the bronze serpent and Christ, these liftings are a key part of the process of healing. In Numbers 21:8-9, the people must look up to the serpent lifted on the pole in order to be healed from their snake bites, and Jesus must be lifted on the cross to heal the relationship between God and humanity. In both of these accounts, the people are not able to heal themselves, but God heals the people through God's own power. In both cases, God's power is shown in the healing that results from the one who is lifted.

Poole and Wesley follow John 3:15 in drawing an analogy between the people who look up to the bronze serpent and those believing in Christ who was lifted on the cross. Thus, as they explain the connections between Numbers 21:8-9 and John 3:14-15, they instruct their readers in the importance of faith in Christ and encourage them to live with trust in God's power to heal their sin through the process of sanctification, in which the Holy Spirit works in Christians by guiding them to live as more faithful disciples of Christ. This example showcases how Wesley emphasizes reflection on Christian teaching and practice in his notes.

Henry, Poole, and Wesley all discuss the connections between Numbers 21:4-9 and John 3:14-15, but Wesley follows Poole in making an additional connection to Christian teaching in his comments on Numbers 21:5. Since Henry does not include explicit remarks on Christian teaching in his discussion of Numbers 21:5, Wesley, by following Poole, reveals his goal of including even more reflection on Christian teaching than Henry. In his notes on Numbers 21:5, Wesley includes Poole's explanation of the Israelites complaining

"Against God - Against Christ, their chief conductor, whom they tempted." For Poole and Wesley, the Israelites complain specifically against Christ who has been their guide in the wilderness. Poole and Wesley thus encourage their readers to reflect on how they have doubted and complained against Christ their guide. Although Wesley does not include significant additions to Poole's remarks in his notes on Numbers 21:4-9, Wesley's inclusion of Poole's interpretation of Christ guiding the Israelites in Numbers 21:5 exemplifies Wesley's interest in reflections about Christian teaching and practice. By drawing on Poole's comments on Numbers 21:4-9, Wesley demonstrates his emphasis on the benefits of biblical scholarship, accessible resources, and reflection on Christian teaching and practice.

Conclusion

In the Preface to his *Explanatory Notes Upon the Old Testament*, Wesley explains his motivations, processes, and goals. His explanation leads to several lessons for how Christians today can practice Wesleyan biblical interpretation:
1) All Christians are called to search the Scriptures.
2) As Christians seek resources to aid in their growth in discipleship, they can appreciate and utilize works of biblical scholarship.
3) Pastors can follow Wesley's model in guiding their congregations in biblical interpretation in accessible ways.

Wesley's driving motivation for producing his *Explanatory Notes Upon the Old Testament* can be a powerful example for contemporary Christians. Despite the challenges of producing these notes, he persevered because he deeply believed that searching the Scriptures is a means of grace. He recognized that the three—reading, hearing, and meditating on the Scriptures—change the lives of Christians. When Christians study the Scriptures, they encounter God—they grow in knowledge and love of God. This growth leads them to be more faithful disciples of Christ. That power to transform drove Wesley to tackle the daunting obstacles the notes presented him.

Wesley's deep appreciation for the power of meditating on the OT provides an inspiring example for Christians today. His example calls all Christians to recognize the importance of studying Scripture. Wesley implores

Christians to search the Old and New Testaments daily, as he does, and this is a foundational lesson for Wesleyan biblical interpretation today. The first step is to search the Scriptures frequently. Christians can seek out many ways to do this. They can hear them read in worship, read them in individual devotion, meditate on them in small groups, and encounter them in many other contexts. As Christians searching the Scriptures expect to meet God, they find guidance and sustenance for their growth in discipleship. Regularly searching the Scriptures is the beginning of Wesleyan biblical interpretation.

Wesley recognizes the challenges of studying the Scriptures, and like many Christians, he finds the OT more daunting than the NT. Because he recognizes the demands of studying Scripture, he looks for resources that can assist him, and this serves as another vital lesson for Wesleyan biblical interpretation. Wesley encourages Christians to seek resources that can aid their study of Scripture. While emphasizing that Christians should meditate on Scripture itself, Wesley recognizes how helpful additional resources can be for biblical interpretation. He demonstrates this by drawing on the works of Matthew Henry and Matthew Poole to produce his *Explanatory Notes Upon the Old Testament*. Wesley's example invites Christians today to appreciate the work of biblical scholars and to seek resources that can assist them in their study of Scripture.

Wesley's use of Henry's and Poole's work also suggests that not all biblical scholarship may be equally helpful for particular Christians. He provides insights for Christians today in his description of why he chose Henry's and Poole's work and how he used each one. Wesley selected their commentaries because they were models of both piety and extensive learning.

Furthermore, Wesley discerns that parts of Henry's and Poole's work were more helpful than others for his goals. For example, Wesley consciously omitted Henry's comments about "Particular Redemption" because Wesley did not view them as helpful for growth in discipleship. His selective use of Henry's work provides a helpful model for Christians today. Although Wesley chose Henry's work for its many strengths, he identified some parts of Henry's work as more helpful for guiding Christian practice. However, this identification does not diminish his gratitude for the benefits of Henry's work and that of other biblical scholarship. His approach in this respect serves as another helpful lesson for Wesleyan biblical interpretation: even as Christians select authors and works of biblical scholarship that they find helpful for growth in discipleship, they may find some parts of these works more helpful than others, and this need not change their posture of appreciation for biblical scholarship in general. Like Wesley, contemporary Christians can carefully engage the work of biblical scholars while expecting to find some parts of their work more helpful for their journey. Christians today can follow Wesley's example not only by drawing on biblical scholarship but also by doing so with thoughtful discernment. As they experience the benefits of insights from biblical scholarship, Christians can also share Wesley's gratitude for how it contributes to growth in faithful discipleship.

Wesley's explanation of his process of preparing his *Explanatory Notes Upon the Old Testament* reveals his deep concern for Christians having accessible resources—tools that are actually helpful for them in their growth in discipleship. The benefits of accessible resources for Christians are as powerful today as they were in Wesley's time. When Wesley describes his process in producing his notes, he details not only how he prioritizes insights that will help Christians grow in discipleship, but he also makes a number of changes to make his notes a practical resource for Christians with a wide range of educational backgrounds. By making shorter notes written in plainer language, Wesley hopes Christians who do not have the time, education, or financial resources to engage Henry's work directly may find his *Explanatory Notes Upon the Old Testament* beneficial for searching the Scriptures.

Wesley's role in producing such resources can be an example for pastors and other Christian leaders today. He writes frankly about his own feeling of inadequacy to produce a guide to the OT on his own: he confesses his "deep conviction" of his "insufficiency" for this task. Yet, Wesley proceeds anyway, and his method serves as a helpful model for contemporary pastors and other church leaders. He sought out works produced by others who had studied the OT in more depth than he had, and he drew on them as he produced a resource that would benefit many in his ministry context. Wesley also drew on his many conversations with people in his ministry who had less formal education than he did, and he used these experiences to guide him in producing a resource that would be more accessible for many in his context. He did not let his lack of in-depth knowledge of the OT stop him, and he found the resources he needed to achieve his goal. The need to aid those in his ministry context empowered Wesley to find a way through his own limitations.

Pastors and Christian leaders can be empowered by Wesley's example as they guide and equip those in their ministry contexts who search the Scriptures. Equipping those in a ministry context may take many forms—it could include producing more accessible resources as Wesley did, and it could include extending Wesley's impulse to provide practical assistance for studying Scripture even further. Many church leaders have training that equips them to engage with biblical scholarship, and they can draw on it in many aspects of their teaching ministries—in sermons, in Bible studies, in written newsletters or blog posts, and other forms. Like Wesley, pastors' experiences speaking with people in their ministry contexts give them insights into how to communicate effectively with people in those contexts. Because of these experiences, pastors can play a vital role in guiding their ministry context in searching the Scriptures.

Church leaders today may find more ways to guide others in their growth in discipleship through searching the Scriptures. Pastors may know some of the unique needs of people in their ministry contexts, and they can find effective ways to communicate to meet them. While limited time and financial resources may still be concerns, additional challenges may call for more creative solutions today. For example, if some in a ministry context are unable to read, pastors can seek creative ways to engage Scripture in auditory formats that are accessible to those who would benefit from them. Church leaders practice Wesleyan biblical interpretation when they find ways to guide those in their ministry contexts to dive deeper into Scripture.

Wesley's insights in the Preface to his *Explanatory Notes Upon the Old Testament* provide vibrant lessons for Christians who are interested in Wesleyan biblical interpretation today. His understanding of the power of searching the Scriptures for growth in discipleship calls Christians to read, hear, and meditate on the Old and New Testament as often as they can. Wesley's deep gratitude for the work of biblical scholarships provides an example for Christians who seek resources to aid them on their journeys deeper into the Scriptures, and Wesley models how to use these resources with discernment to recognize the parts most beneficial for one's growth in discipleship. Additionally, Wesley's process of producing his notes empowers pastors and Christian leaders today to draw on resources from biblical scholarship as they find effective ways to equip people in their ministry contexts for the transformative work of searching the Scriptures.

References

Jones, Scott. 1995. *John Wesley's Conception and Use of Scripture*. Nashville: Kingswood Books.

Wesley, John. 1975. Explanatory Notes Upon the Old Testament. 3 vols. Salem, OH: Schmul Publishers.

———. "Free Grace" (Sermon 128). Wesley Center Online. http://wesley.nnu.edu/john-wesley/the-sermons-of-john-wesley-1872-edition/sermon-128-free-grace/.

———. "The Means of Grace" (Sermon 16). Wesley Center Online. http://wesley.nnu.edu/john-wesley/the-sermons-of-john-wesley-1872-edition/sermon-16-the-means-of-grace/.

For Further Reading

Casto, Robert Michael. 1977. "Exegetical Method in John Wesley's *Explanatory Notes Upon the Old Testament*." PhD dissertation, Durham: Duke University.

Maddox, Randy. 2011. "The Rule of Christian Faith, Practice, and Hope: John Wesley on the Bible." *Methodist Review* 3: 1–35.

Schlimm, Matthew. 2007. "Defending the Old Testament's Worth: John Wesley's Reaction to the Rebirth of Marcionism." *Wesleyan Theological Journal* 42 no. 7: 28–51.

CHAPTER 7

Drawn from the Waters
A Wesleyan Interpretation of New Birth in Exodus 2:1-10 in Conversation with Philosophical Hermeneutics

Kristin Helms

In October 2019, The United Methodist Church was on the verge of splitting. The bishop of the Greater New Jersey Annual Conference formed a task force in order to create ways to preserve unity in the midst of strong opposing forces. At a Special Annual Conference session, everyone gathered to consider the task force's proposal, and a rule was suggested for the deliberations: no one was to refer to the Bible to support their positions. This was not because people thought the Bible was unimportant, but rather because it was believed that anyone on any side could use the Bible to make their point equally well, rendering all interpretations irrelevant for discerning God's will moving forward. Eventually, when someone in the conference did refer to the Bible, he was rebuffed with a well-intentioned rebuke from another conference member: "I would just like to remind the body that we were instructed earlier . . . not to use the Bible as a means of saying one is more correct than the other. We all have different interpretations of Scripture . . . We are not all of one mind on how to read the Bible. Therefore, I just remind the body:

Please do not use your interpretation of what the Bible says to be the correct one" (Caulfield 2019). This statement demonstrates the current philosophical climate in which Methodists live in the United States. Sally has her interpretation of the Bible; Bob has his interpretation of the Bible; they can only speak constructively with people who already agree with them, and so the Bible cannot correct or hold anyone accountable, because we accept that we cannot agree on what it means.

People tend to draw conclusions about what the Bible means based upon their experiences, practical personal concerns, and how they have been trained to interpret Scripture through their years of education at church and in school. Amid the plurality of competing interests, there persists an utter inability of people to talk to one another congenially and productively. However, this common occurrence is also related, I submit, to broad, cultural *philosophical* undercurrents that govern our dialogue. Such is not only happening in the church. These undercurrents make difficult conversations seemingly impossible (Ellison 2017). Our (often unspoken) philosophical assumptions create barriers to authentic and productive communication.

When God's people can no longer use the Bible, of all things, to discern God's will in community, and when God's people who are theologically educated cannot speak the philosophical languages of the world around them enough to engage it constructively, then it is clearly time for some self-assessment. It is time for the Methodist movement to pay attention to the philosophical forces at work in the minds of people within our culture. For our purposes we must acknowledge the way those forces influence our interpretations of the Bible. Moreover, for our focus on Wesleyan biblical interpretation in particular, it is important to consider John Wesley's engagements with philosophy in relation to his biblical interpretation.

Wesley, Philosophy, and the "Plain Meaning of Scripture"

Wesley's use of philosophy in his interpretation of Scripture is a relatively neglected topic in Wesleyan studies. There are some very good reasons for this. For one, people are rarely attracted to Wesley out of a love for reading philosophy. They are drawn to Wesley's fiery passion for the love of God and others, his relentless dedication to revival, and his moving ways of speaking about God's saving grace. As a result, philosophy can come across as disconnected from the heart of the Methodist movement he inspired. Methodist denominations do not require training in philosophy for ordination or other forms of church leadership. Indeed, while Wesley himself was incredibly well read in philosophy, he did not think it was for everyone. He certainly did not explicitly reflect upon his own "biblical hermeneutics" for others to consider, in part because he would rather just *do it* and find others who could do it well for the sake of inspiring holiness. There is another significant reason, though, that John Wesley himself did not write much about the relationship between philosophy and his interpretation of the Bible: in his context, he could presume a "plain meaning of Scripture." While people might argue about this or that interpretation, his approach was more or less consistent with the type of approach used around him such that it was not common to seriously contest the idea that a "plain" or "literal" meaning of the text existed.

In what follows I do not attempt to give a full-scale account of Wesleyan philosophical approaches to biblical studies, as that would be a project far beyond the scope of a single chapter. Rather, here I wish to simply raise the issue and, in very broad strokes, to provide an accessible example of biblical interpretation that takes seriously both its Wesleyan heritage and the philosophical undercurrents within our culture generally speaking. For philosophy lovers, the general way in which I discuss the philosophies will inevitably leave a lot to be desired. Nonetheless, my modest objective is simply to inspire Christians in the Wesleyan tradition to engage in conversation regarding the relationship between Wesleyan biblical interpretation and the popular philosophical movements that shape our work of making disciples.

Exodus 2:1-10 and New Birth

As a biological mother, a foster parent, and a friend of women who have faced infertility, I have often drawn on the story of Moses's birth and adoption in Exodus 2:1-10 to explain concepts of "new birth" to people. Now, John Wesley was not a fan of figurative interpretation, given that such deviates from the "plain" meaning of the text. Yet I maintain that I indeed act as a good Wesleyan when I use the Moses story in this way. No doubt, from the perspective of Wesley himself, John 3:5-6 is a better, more true-to-the-text Scripture to use for that purpose, since Exodus 2:1-10 is about literal birth and adoption rather than spiritual birth and adoption.[1] That said, I am not being fancifully typological when I use this text. Exodus 2:1-10 is related to the message of John 3:5-6 from both a historical and canonical perspective. The ancient Near Eastern imagery in the text most certainly presents Moses's adoption as a second birth, as I discuss in detail below.

The birth story of Moses also textually foreshadows the birth of the nation of Israel that will happen to an already-existing people group as they pass through the Sea in Exodus 14 (Fretheim 1990, 38–41). Just as Moses is saved from the waters by a second birth—adoption—so also Israel is saved from the waters by a second birth. This story of the Exodus event in Exodus 1–15 becomes the paradigmatic portrayal of *what new birth means* for the entire rest of the Bible and into the Christian tradition of baptism. Indeed, given John's significant use of Exodus in this Gospel, when Jesus tells Nicodemus that everyone must be born of water and the Spirit, it is most certainly appropriate to view these words against the backdrop of these chapters in Exodus (Foster 2017). In short, to use Exodus 2:1-10 is not a poetic, ornamental leap, but it is rather true to the literary context, the ancient Near Eastern imagery, and way in which the tenor of the Bible itself and the Christian tradition understand the Exodus event.

Straying somewhat even further from "the plain meaning of the text," I admit that I have used Exodus 2:1-10 in church contexts to talk about how, from a biblical perspective, effective evangelism should look a bit similar to women giving birth. Again, there are many other biblical texts that explicitly talk about evangelism; but, again, I think this text has something to offer the conversation. The "new birth" imagery runs deep within all Christian traditions, and it is central within the Wesleyan tradition.[2] Yet, when I look at many evangelism efforts, I am not always sure those efforts resonate with

---

1. For example, note Wesley's preference for John 3:5-6 in his sermon "The New Birth" (Sermon 45).

2. According to Robert Wall, "No part is more strategic to Wesley's soteriology than the doctrine of new birth; no reading of Scripture can escape its impress. The believer's regeneration is the lynchpin that holds justification by faith and one's 'present, inward salvation' together" (Wall 2012, 44).

the same level of total self-giving and sacrifice that happens to the mothers in the Exodus story. What would it even mean for evangelism to look like giving birth, biblically speaking? What imagery in this text might be useful in considering how to make disciples well?

Wesley's primary concern, with regard to straying from literal language, was a concern that interpretation be grounded in the divine revelation of the Bible rather than in the potentially fallible imagination of the interpreter (Shelton 1981). He only advocated for a figurative reading of a text when the literal reading was nonsensical. In what I have said so far, I hope it is apparent that biblical interpretation should be accountable to the text. However—and this is where attention to philosophical perspectives comes in—I also believe metaphors are important to our understanding of the literal meaning of the text itself. An ancient Near Eastern reader of Exodus 2:1-10 would hear the literal meaning of the text substantially differently than someone in my culture. Indeed, from an ancient perspective, Moses is really and truly born twice in this text, which is nonsense from a literal reading of the text that arises out of my own contemporary community. The philosophical approach of Conceptual Metaphor Theory (CMT), which was pioneered by George Lakoff and Mark Turner (1989), Paul Ricoeur (2003), and George Lakoff and Mark Johnson (2008), and developed long after the time of Wesley, is what convinced me of this. Understanding the value of CMT for contemporary biblical interpretation requires a little bit of knowledge about its relationship to philosophical trajectories since the time of René Descartes and their impact upon biblical interpretation.

A Very Brief Sketch of Philosophical Trajectories Since Descartes

Descartes (1596–1650) wondered how much of what he thought he was experiencing in the world was actually real. After all, sometimes people hallucinate or wake up from a dream in which they thought they were, say, by the fire, but actually the fire died long ago. If this can happen, how can people ever really know that what they think they are experiencing truly exists? At any moment the senses may be tricked. There was one thing, however, that he could believe with indelible certainty: he was definitely thinking about these things. Therefore, he must exist. In other words, the one certainty for him was this: "I think therefore I am." With that thought began a massive philosophical shift in terms of understanding what we can really know to be true.

Prior to Descartes, Christians and non-Christians alike believed in something along the lines of a "first cause" of all things. As the originator of everything else, everything in the universe finds its meaning in that first cause. In Christian terms, creation derives its meaning from its Creator, because it is from the Creator that all things come into existence. In the centuries following Descartes, great skepticism grew as to what anyone could know apart from one's own logic. "I" became the center from which I must construct my understanding of everything else, because I am the only sure thing. In the end, my (the individual's) reason is understood to be my only access to truth, and it can only safely be understood as a subjective truth, because I have no certain knowledge of what is happening outside of myself. So, if there is a first cause, I cannot know for sure that I know what it is. To claim otherwise is to project onto the world outside of myself and claim that I know something great that I could never know from my small, limited, relative position.

Once fully grown, this eventually yields postmodernity. Of course, the leap from Descartes to postmodernity did not happen overnight, nor was he its only line of contribution. There were other significant shifts from various influential thinkers. One vital shift was the advent of the natural sciences. At first the natural sciences remained philosophically connected to the idea of a Creator, studying that creation and marveling at the manner in which its sheer organization and logic pointed to a logical Being at its origins. Eventually, though, the logic itself began to be viewed as superior to God in the sense that God was viewed to be acting on logical principles that existed independently of any Creator. Martin de Mersenne (1588–1648), for example, argued that math was not an invention of God but rather exists as an "eternal truth" in its own right. Human reason could, therefore, skip theology and go straight to the study of those eternal truths to which even God was bound. John Locke (1632–1704) famously argued for an approach of seeking knowledge through what our bodies' physical senses can experience.

During the Enlightenment, other notable philosophers rallied people to shake off the shackles of authorities—who tell you what to believe—and learn to use reason to think for yourself. Immanuel Kant (1724–1804) believed God remained a useful category insofar as a notion of the divine inspires morality; but, apart from ethics, for him, there was no need for God in society. Moreover, he argued that the existence of God cannot be proven by reason, and so it is not possible to know that God exists. Karl Marx (1818–1883) noted that powerful people had used the idea of God to justify exploiting people economically and socially. Eventually, Friedrich Nietzsche (1844–1900) declared, "God is dead."

John Wesley (1703–1791) lived toward the beginning of the Enlightenment, and the implications of all these thoughts were not yet fully developed. He incorporated ideas especially from Descartes and Locke into his theology, disagreeing with them when their thoughts violated theological ideas that he believed to be true. Philosophy remained a tool in the practice of Wesley, as a servant rather than master of divine revelation. Randy Maddox suggests that, for Wesley, reason "was not another source of revelation supplementing that of creation or the Bible, it was the 'candle of the Lord' given to help us appropriate revelation. Its value lay in its ability to provide responsible (i.e., publicly defensible) interpretations and applications of God's gracious revelation in nature and Scripture." (Maddox 1994, 41). In his sermon, "The Case of Reason Impartially Considered (Sermon 70)," Wesley argues that it is important not to fall into an extreme of overvaluing reason to the point of viewing it as infallible nor into the extreme of undervaluing reason to the point that it is deemed to have no value for understanding the world and even divine revelation. That said, Wesley never engaged in conversations about how these philosophies might affect the study of the Bible itself, still sharing a view with those around him that the plain, literal message of the Bible was a given (Green 2012).

The postmodern landscape in which we live and do ministry, however, is very different. Rather than speaking about one great truth, people in postmodernity are now commonly far more comfortable with limited, self-determined truths that derive from one's own experience and understanding. Likewise, many people in postmodernity find talking about one literal, plain meaning of a text—any text—to be impossibly unrealistic, because everyone will see what they see in the text based upon their own individual experiences. It is viewed to be elitist, inappropriately authoritarian, potentially exploitative, and arrogant to suggest that one's own interpretation is the one true interpretation. Thus, no one can publicly claim that a particular interpretation of the Bible is the only interpretation. It is challenging to even find a means outside of the individual's own opinion to determine which interpretation is best in a broad, diverse community.

A consequence of all of this is a radical and even isolating focus upon the individual. Community is difficult when we can and must all have our own truths. Rather than one big community that can encompass everyone, people gravitate in this environment to little communities that resonate with their experiences and with which they can personally agree. In other words, whereas in Wesley's time theological disagreements across party lines looked like arguing over what the Bible *really says*, today they look like dismissing conversations about such disagreements altogether. It is a complicated environment in which to share the gospel, insofar as Jesus makes truth claims upon all people.

However, postmodernity has also been a fruitful and rich environment for learning to respect the many different ways in which people experience the Christian life and the biblical text. A drawback to John Wesley's worldview was a sort of heavy-handedness to what the Bible was allowed to mean. In postmodernity, in contrast, there is an openness to hear many possible fresh things from God within the biblical text and to think about how that works. But the question remains: is it possible for people to talk constructively, and even persuasively, with people who completely disagree with their reading of the Bible and who settle into a "this is my truth" mindset?

Cognitive Metaphor Theory (CMT)

Here is where the approaches from the phenomenological family of philosophy, such as CMT, are helpful. The rally cry of phenomenology, as first developed by Edmund Husserl (1859–1938), is "back to the thing itself." This does not mean a return to the thing outside of one's self with the belief that one can ever know something apart from one's own limited experience of it. It is, however, a recognition that I have experiences of a real world outside of myself, and Emmanuel Lévinas (1906–1995) beautifully demonstrated the ethical accountability to respect and serve what "I" experience apart from myself as an Other. CMT, following the metaphorical theory initially developed by Paul Ricoeur (1917–2005), is related to this strand of thought. It suggests that the way in which "I" make sense out of that Other apart from myself is through metaphors. In other words, metaphors are not just beautiful or creative ways of saying something, but rather they help us conceptualize reality.

CMT contends that metaphors actually pervade our conceptualizations of the world in many areas of life. For example, what is "time"? Whether you are a scientist or a theologian or painter, American culture tends to understand time on the basis of the conceptual metaphor, "time is money." Lakoff and Johnson demonstrate that "time is money" constructs the way we speak and thus learn to think about time on a very deep level. Consider some common phrases: "How do you *spend* your time these days?" "That flat tire *cost* me an hour." "I've *invested* a lot of time in her." "You're *running out* of time." "You don't use your time *profitably*" (Lakoff and Johnson 2008, 8). You can even post bail with money—or serve time in jail, as if the money and time are interchangeable. Speaking and acting in this way in our culture habituates us into thinking of time through the lens of money. This lens allows us to see certain things about time that we deem to be true to our experience of time. It is an important and limited resource. As Lakoff and Turner put it, "Metaphor resides in thought, not just in words" (Lakoff and Turner 1989, 2).

At the same time, time is not *really* money. That is why it is a metaphor. Because time is not really money, the metaphor is only true to a point. There is thus a limit beyond which money no longer serves as a useful conceptual framework to understand time. For example, unlike money, all people at any given moment have exactly the same amount of that particular moment. Once a moment in time is "spent," we cannot get that time back in the same way that money shuffles around through the economy. Thus, money is not a helpful framework for conceptualizing time in all regards. It is useful and typical then to have other major metaphors to help one think about other aspects of time hidden by the "time is money" metaphor. One such alternative metaphor in our culture is "time is a moving object": "Time *flies*!" "The time *will come* when . . ." "The time has long since *gone* when . . ." "The time *has arrived*!" "Before us is a great opportunity, and we don't want it to *pass us by*" (Lakoff and Johnson 2008, 41–44). This metaphor is better than "time is money" in conceptualizing time in certain ways, such as the way in which time cannot be "earned back." The two metaphors supplement each other, and our language and thought need both to help us to conceptualize what time *is* in a way that is true to the fullest extent of how we experience time.

For this reason, when we hit a limit in our understanding, new metaphors can be powerful in finding alternative paths of thought. Donald Schön (1930–1997) gives a helpful example of this in his classic article, "Generative Metaphor and Social Policy." He tells about a group of researchers who had the task of improving the synthetic-bristle paintbrush. The synthetic-bristle brush was leaving a gloppy paint finish as opposed to the smooth finish of a natural-bristle paintbrush. The researchers were charged with fixing the problem (Schön 1993, 142–43). They were not having a lot of luck. They tried different diameters for the synthetic bristles. They tried splitting the ends of the bristles in the manner of the natural bristles. Still, the paint came out gloppy. Then one of the researchers had a breakthrough: "*A paintbrush is a kind of pump.*" In other words, as in the case of a pump, the paint was carried not by the bristles but by *the space between* the bristles, and when the bristles were pressed against a surface, the bristles "pumped" the paint through the "channels" of that space. This new metaphor enabled the researchers to see the difference between the natural and synthetic bristles that was resulting in the smooth versus gloppy finish. *That difference had been right in front of their eyes the entire time, but it took the new metaphor to enable them to perceive it.* Notice that the metaphor was not distracting the researchers from what was truly happening with the paintbrushes in an amusing or dismissively ornamental manner, which might distract them from what was literally happening with the paintbrush, but it rather enabled them to see the phenomenon more clearly.

The Birth of Moses Meets Conceptual Metaphor Theory

With this in mind, let us return to the matter of birth and rebirth introduced above. Consider that the conceptual metaphorical framework that our society uses to describe childbirth belongs almost exclusively to the realm of biology, largely because of the role medicine plays in childbirth in our culture.

Most women in our culture go to medical professionals at some point within the childbirth process even when they are healthy, and even when they do not, they usually feel like they should.

Medicine has long used the conceptual metaphor, "the womb is a machine." Consider, for example, this quote from a prominent gynecology textbook in the mid-1980s:

> Labor is work; mechanically, work is the generation of motion against resistance. The forces involved in labor are those of the uterus and the abdomen that act to expel the fetus and that must overcome the resistance offered by the cervix to dilation and the friction created by the birth canal during passage of the presenting part (Pritchard, MacDonald, and Grant 1985, 331).

This quotation describes the process of labor in childbirth in entirely mechanical terms. The "presenting part" is the baby. In this mechanical metaphor, the uterus does the work. Remarkably, there is no reference to the mother as a person at all.

The medical metaphor, "the body is a machine," which makes childbirth the work of the machine, has many useful purposes. However, since the 1980s medical professionals have increasingly noticed that treating the female womb as if it is *just* a machine sometimes does not benefit the health and well-being of the mother and baby. This is understandable, as this illustration from Nancy Cohen and Lois Estner demonstrates:

> If your husband was told that he had to get an erection and ejaculate . . . perhaps he could have an I.V. put in his arm, be kept in one position, have straps placed around his penis, and be told not to move: He could be checked every few minutes; the sheet could be lifted to see if any "progress" had been made (Cohen and Estner 1983, 173).

As would be the case if healthy men were normally treated this way, so also medical professionals increasingly acknowledge that high levels of mechanical intervention throughout a healthy female's labor and delivery process can do more harm than good. It is the failure to recognize the limits of a *metaphorical* understanding of the womb.

As a result, while the "womb is a machine" metaphor has definitely not disappeared, nor should it, over the past couple of decades in our culture it has become regularly supplemented with social service metaphors. Social services, such as counseling, provide support to persons as they go through a challenging period. Giving birth is often experienced as painful and as physically exhausting by the mother, and the medical professional offers a type of "social service" for her as she labors and gives birth. This supplementary metaphor enables health care providers to see what is happening in birth in a fuller sort of way than they could through the lens of the former mechanical metaphors alone, even as they continue to view the female body also through the lens of medicine's more basic conceptual metaphors. Working together, the truths that each metaphor reveals has allowed for better birth experiences and outcomes.

However, these metaphors still have limits, particularly from a pastoral perspective. What do these metaphors say about a woman who cannot physically reproduce? She is a broken machine. She is someone who fails despite the best efforts of social services. Consider also, from a different angle, what do these metaphors say about the woman who wants to give birth but never has the opportunity to do so? She simply *cannot* give birth according to our conceptual understanding of birth. However, recall that when someone hits the limits of one conceptual metaphor, supplementing that metaphor with another powerful, conceptual metaphor can empower a breakthrough in understanding, as in the paint brush analogy mentioned above. A new generative metaphor can enable us to see new aspects of the experience of reality that are already there but that we cannot see from just one metaphorical perspective, just as "time is money" does not reveal everything about the experience of time, and "time is a moving object" helps to supplement it. In our case, an additional metaphor from a different culture that views birth in a different way can generate new conceptualizations of maternity and childbirth, highlighting aspects of birth that are already there but that we cannot presently see. The birth story of Moses, when read in its ancient Near Eastern context, offers such a supplementary metaphor.

The imagery of birth that surrounds the mother and the adopting mother in Exodus 2:1–10 presents birth not through the lens of a mechanical metaphor nor through the lens of a social service metaphor but rather through the lens of the theological metaphor, "Childbirth is creation." For example, when the mother bears the child in Exodus 2:2, it says, "She saw that he was good" (Author's Translation). This echoes the first thing on God's mind after he makes each part of creation in Genesis 1:1–2:4, "He saw that it was good.". Other echoes back to the Genesis creation story like this occur throughout the book of Exodus. For example, in the beginning of Exodus we see that what will be Moses's childbirth in Exodus 2:2 is just one of many, many births taking place among the Hebrew people, as they "<u>were fruitful</u> and prolific; they <u>multiplied</u>" and "<u>the land was filled with them</u>" (Exod. 1:7). This directly echoes the language in Gen. 1:28, which says "<u>be fruitful</u> and <u>multiply</u>, and <u>fill</u> the earth."

The echo shows the reader that Hebrew people were to the utmost fulfilling God's blessing upon humanity to be fruitful. Moses's birth appears as this prolific period of baby-making blessing is creating a situation that troubles their master, the Egyptian Pharaoh. The Pharaoh of Egypt experiences anxiety and alarm at the sheer number of Hebrew babies and their ever-growing strength. Fearing them as he notes that they might one day be powerful enough to fight against the Egyptian people, he sets out to destroy the male babies. His cruel acts include ordering that the midwives throw all newborn boys into the Nile River. This sets the context. The Egyptian Pharaoh makes himself the opponent of the Creator's blessing of making many babies.

The creation imagery continues through the remainder of Exodus 2:3-10, in which Moses is both placed into and drawn out of the waters that are the Egyptian king's planned means of murder. There is a relationship between water and creation throughout the Old Testament and in ancient Near Eastern literature. Most such creation stories start the depiction of the yet-to-be-formed cosmos as a place of dark waters. In Genesis 1:3-13 the very first acts of creation describe God *limiting* the realm of the watery darkness described in Genesis 1:2. Only after God has limited the dark waters and there exists a bright, dry, breathable space, can new creations, including humans, come into existence (Gen. 1:14-31). In other words, creation depends upon and requires the limiting of the dark, primeval waters.

Other biblical texts recall this limiting of the primeval waters as an important step in creation, as well (e.g., Ps. 104:9; Prov. 8:29). One interesting example of this is Job 38:4-10, in which God challenges Job with the words:

"Where were you when I laid the foundation of the earth? . . . Who shut in the sea with its doors when it burst out from the <u>womb</u> . . . and said, 'Thus far shall you come and no farther, and here shall your proud waves be stopped.'" ..

This middle verse in that passage (Job 38:8) may sound odd to us, because it connects the limits of the sea with the *womb*, and we are not accustomed to thinking in this way. However, the imagery Job 3:8 is using here helps us to see a correlation that existed in ancient Near Eastern cultures, metaphorically linking creation (including the limiting of the primeval waters) with childbirth. The metaphor in play here is not "childbirth is a mechanical process" or "childbirth is a hard time requiring social services," but rather "<u>childbirth is a reenactment of the creation</u>." For a new baby to exist, the waters from the realm in which he/she cannot exist must encounter a limit, so to speak. That limit, set by God, is the female body. As the baby is formed within the womb, the mother's body functions as a sort of boat that protects the baby from the waters and ultimately delivers him or her into the port of life, enabling safe passage into creation.

We can see this all the more clearly when we look at texts that give us a glimpse into the birth language of the ancient Near Eastern cultures that influenced the language of the text. One example of this is found in an Old Babylonian birth incantation, which begins with a description of conception, in which the parents' "waters" intermingle, proceeds to the stage of pregnancy, throughout which the baby is surrounded by dark, raging, "far off" ocean waters, and then moves on to labor, at which point the path to the door of the womb is divinely opened, and then finally delivery, in which the womb opens so the baby can come out (Stol 2009, 143). Deliverance from the waters is, indeed, essential to what childbirth *is* from this perspective.

We also find ancient Near Eastern texts that speak of the mother's body as the "ship" in the process of "sailing" the baby safely to the quay of life, where the mother's muscles will need to relax well in order to "drop off" the baby (Bermann 2008, 27). Interestingly, in the mechanical metaphor of our culture, we tend to think about the need for the mother's muscles to have strong *contractions*. It is well known, though, that *relaxation* is also a significant factor in delivering a baby. This text speaks of "relaxing" the muscles so that the ship (the woman's body) may be loosened and the new, separate human form may come forth to see light of life.

In sum, the cultures surrounding the Hebrew people drew a metaphorical connection between childbirth and creation, with the mother being the physical vessel that delivered the new creation from the dark waters. When we read the story of Exodus in light of the knowledge of these common ancient metaphors, "childbirth is creation" and "the female body is the boat," we can see them at work in the story of Moses's *adoption*, presenting it as a second experience of birth. First, consider the use of the waters to kill the babies in the context of the story. Within this story that contains so many allusions to creation, notice that throwing the babies into the waters in effect reverses the creation process for those baby boys. If the women deliver the babies out of the waters into life, so now the king requires his people to throw the babies back into waters.

When Moses's Hebrew mother gives birth to Moses, however, she cannot bring herself to do this. Instead, she builds a basket. The Hebrew word for basket here is a relatively rare word, *tēbah*, that means "boat." Interestingly, given the numerous explicit echoes to creation imagery in these early chapters of Exodus, the only other biblical place in the Bible that we find this Hebrew word is the story of Noah and the "ark" (*tēbah*).[3] In the story of Noah's ark, "the windows of the heavens were opened" (Gen. 7:11) to allow the primeval waters to overflow the dry ground again, and all the creations that live therein drown in the waters. It is an act that reverses the creation in Genesis 1:1-2:4. However, God saves Noah, his family, and the animals through the *tēbah* (ark/boat). The *tēbah* becomes the safe place delivering some of the creatures from the waters for the sake of re-establishing a new creation on the other side

---

3. I do not intend to suggest that Exodus 2 is necessarily echoing the flood story intentionally so much as to point out that both ancient use in the ancient concepts of the waters and the *tēbah* to the ends of discussing the ending of a creation and the establishment of a new creation, albeit each in their own ways and for their own purposes. This demonstrates the enduring nature of the metaphorical connection across texts. All the more, with regard to the commonly discussed J and P schema of authorship for the flood narrative in Genesis 6–9, the rare word *tēbah* is consistent in verses attributed to both J and to P. If a J, E, D, P conceptualization of authorship is accurate, this further highlights the endurance of these terms being linked to these uncreation/new creation concepts across periods of composition.

of the event.[4] So also in Moses's birth story, the king orders that the Hebrew baby boys drown in the waters. Moses is delivered from drowning in the waters through a *tēbah*, often translated into English as "basket" in this context. Moses lives because of this safe place that delivers him from the waters. If we read the birth of Moses not with our own mechanical view of childbirth but rather through the lens of creation in which the female body is the boat that safely delivers and protects a new baby as he or she passes through those waters, then we can see that what the birth mother is doing here is placing her baby *back into the waters in a new boat*. On the other side of this act is the possibility for Moses to be reestablished as part of the creation. In other words, the mother obeys the king's order to put the baby (back) into the waters, but she does so in such a way as to open an opportunity to save the baby from the waters . . . again.

At this point, the king's daughter comes into the story, and this time *she* draws him out of the waters. The text's language emphasizes this particular point, and by this point underscores the adoption of Moses as a second birth, a second creation, a second deliverance from the waters of un-creation. The text's centralized focus on this point cannot be clearer. The name "Moses" is related to a Hebrew verb meaning "to draw out." (Interestingly, it is also related to an Egyptian word that means "to birth"). Pharaoh's daughter clarifies that she chooses to name the baby Moses, "because *I drew him out of the waters*" (Exod. 2:10). Normally the naming of a child in a birth story takes place right after the birth, and in this story the baby is named right after the king's daughter takes him into her home as her son. In all of these ways the text emphasizes the *identity* of Moses as being one who was birthed, in a very real sense, through his adoption by the daughter of Pharaoh, understood in terms of being drawn out of the waters.

Thus, ancient Near Eastern creation imagery saturates the language used in Exodus 2:1-10 to depict both the first birth and the adoption of Moses. Moses's natural birth and Moses's adoption are acts of creation and new creation. What if the metaphor "birth is creation," drawn from this text, were to

---

4. After the flood God makes a covenant with Noah that, through repeated echoes to Genesis 1–2, establishes him as the New Adam (e.g., Gen. 9:1-2 //1:28; 9:6-7 //1:26-28 // Gen. 3:1–24.).

supplement the mechanical and social service metaphors that we use in our culture to conceptualize birth? For example, at the level of the actual physical woman, I have used this in numerous pastoral situations to help women who cannot give birth biologically to reconceptualize their bodies as still capable of giving birth, very truly, through adoption. I have used this to reconceptualize my sometimes-ambiguous role as foster mom with the numerous children who have come into our home through the years.

However, I also think this metaphor can be used to help the church conceptualize the practice of making disciples, understood in the full Wesleyan sense of spreading scriptural holiness, which has been the primary concern of the Methodist movement from its beginnings. "New birth" is such a common metaphor that people can become numb to its implications for how to bring it about. Exodus 2:1-10, when read through the lens of ancient Near Eastern metaphors, offers an exegetically relevant check on our practices. I have sometimes seen evangelistic efforts that are *only* based upon conceptions of birth that we find in our own culture, often a mix between a mechanical or social-services sort of approach to understanding birth. For example, a Christian community may feel like they are not as healthy as they would like to be in their evangelistic practices, and so they call upon an expert in sharing faith to serve as a doctor of sorts to help them perform in a more healthy way, providing them somewhat mechanically but also supportively with what to say, how to share their testimonies, the statistics on how likely a person is to try out and ultimately join the community under this or that situation, the demographics of the community, adjustments to relevant meeting spaces, etc. There is much good that can come from this, just as there is much good that can come from childbirth under the care of a well-trained medical specialist. However, because it is a metaphor, there are limits to the degree to which it can be helpful. Other explicit metaphors are necessary to prevent accidentally stifling the effectiveness of all this work, given that the realities involved in what effective evangelism is exceeds the limits of the contemporary metaphors undergirding this practice.

The metaphor "childbirth is creation," especially as viewed through the adoption imagery of Exodus 2:1-10, is rich with potential to supplement these contemporary cultural metaphors of birth. Christian communities are called to "adopt" people into their family. The biblical imagery here is one of drawing people out of the cold, dark waters of the world that will drown them, *being the limit* that those deadly waters cannot pass. It is imagery that underscores how impossible it is to deliver other people to new life if we are just another place where people encounter those waters. Pharaoh's daughter has to take the opposite position of the most powerful man in the kingdom, who also happens to be her father in a very patriarchal culture, in order to save baby Moses. She does it because she cares when she looks maternally at this crying child who has no other hope (Exod. 2:6). Moses's two options are adoption/second birth or death. If there is need for a "medical professional" to address ineffective faith-sharing from this perspective, it might be for the purpose of addressing—with the fiery, holy passion akin to that of John Wesley—the need for people to *become* a community that is not actually drowning in the waters of the world itself, a community that can say no to the water's power.

Conclusion

I have tried in this chapter to provide an example of explicitly using a philosophical method for textual interpretation that is respectful of the concerns found in postmodernity and is true to the heart of what it means to be Wesleyan. In closing, I would like to address the issue of interpretive limits. How might a Wesleyan community determine whether or not an interpretation of Scripture is "Wesleyan" in this sort of postmodern climate? In practice, every individual Wesleyan group must draw their own conclusions, since Wesley himself left behind no authoritative group akin to something like the Catholic magisterium to arbitrate such matters for the Methodist. That said, I would argue that my own interpretation here is Wesleyan, based upon some commonly accepted principles.

First, Wesley himself kept up with philosophy and used it as a tool so far as it helped him understand and communicate Christian theology effectively. Second, he advocated for the Analogy of Faith (the biblical outline of original sin, justification, new birth, and sanctification) to guide him in understanding specific biblical texts in terms of the whole tenor of Scripture. If an interpretation of a text violated this Analogy of Faith, he deemed the interpretation to be necessarily inaccurate. Third, Wesley's Anglican background combined with extensive readings of the Early Church fathers provided further theological limits to help navigate difficult biblical passages (e.g., valid biblical interpretations would not go against the orthodox Christian understanding of the Trinity). Fourth, the aim of the Methodist movement was "to spread scriptural holiness and reform the Church of England." My interpretation of Exodus 2:1-10 respects and stands firmly within the theological landscape of these principles, and it is even fueled by these principles, despite making use of a philosophical approach more connected to today.

Importantly, when college students come into my classroom, this method of interpretation allows me to speak to them as they are, with a whole host of postmodern convictions. When *any* Christian today preaches a sermon, offers pastoral guidance, leads a Bible study, organizes a group for mission, or does any other act of ministry, we *all* are interacting with a world with postmodern convictions of varying flavors. It is simply prudent to seek to understand how those convictions frame what people hear and to use approaches that can speak truthfully and faithfully to those convictions in a way that is effective.

References

Bergmann, Claudia D., 2008. *Childbirth as Metaphor for Crisis: Evidence from the Ancient Near East, the Hebrew Bible, and 1 QH XI, 1-18. Beihefte zur Zeitshcrift für die alttestamentliche Wissenshaft*. Berlin: De Gruyter.

Caulfield, Beth. 2019. "Word has really spread. People from all over the world keep asking me if the 3 minutes recorded here at The United Methodist Church Greater New Jersey Special Annual Conference on October 26 really happened." Facebook, November 8, 2019. https://www.facebook.com/beth.caulfield.7/posts/pfbid06PnryfLaenS34SxxqUXDWW9zPNqecu1H W9NRKT2YjbB6iVZXg78wNYDxyJzBxGVsl.

Cohen, Nancy Wainer and Lois J. Estner. 1983. *Silent Knife: Cesarean Prevention and Vaginal Birth After Cesarean (VBAC)* South Hadley, MA: Bergin and Garvey.

Ellison II, Gregory C. 2017. *Fearless Dialogues: A New Movement for Justice*. Minneapolis: Westminster John Knox Press.

Fretheim, Terence E. 1991. *Exodus*. Interpretation. Louisville: Westminster John Knox Press.

Foster, Timothy D. 2017. "John 3:5: Redefining the People of God," *Bulletin for Biblical Research* 27: 351–60.

Green, Joel B. 2012. "Wesley as Interpreter of Scripture and the Emergence of 'History' in Biblical Interpretation." In *Wesley, Wesleyans, and Reading Bible as Scripture*, edited by Joel B. Green and David F. Watson, 47–62. Waco: Baylor University Press.

Lakoff, George and Mark Turner. 1989. *More than Cool Reason: A Field Guide to Poetic Metaphor*. Chicago: University of Chicago Press.

——— 2008. *Metaphors We Live By*. Chicago: University of Chicago Press.

Maddox, Randy. 1994. *Responsible Grace: John Wesley's Practical Theology*. Nashville: Abingdon Press.

Martin, Emily. 1987. *The Woman in the Body: A Cultural Analysis of Reproduction*. Boston: Beacon Press.

Pritchard, Jack A., Paul C. MacDonald, and Norman F. Gant. 1985. *Williams Obstetrics*. 17th edition. Norwalk, CT: Appleton-Century-Crofts.

Ricoeur, Paul. 2003. *The Rule of Metaphor: The Creation of Meaning in Language*. Third edition. New York: Routledge.

Schön, Donald. 1993. "Generative Metaphor: A Perspective on Problem-Setting in Social Policy." In *Metaphor and Thought*, 2nd edition, edited by Andrew Ortony, 137–63. New York: Cambridge University Press.

Shelton, Larry. 1981. "John Wesley's Approach to Scripture in Historical Perspective." *Wesleyan Theological Journal*, 16 (Spring): 23–50.

Stol, Marten. 2009. "Embryology in Babylonia and the Bible." In *Imagining the Fetus: The Unborn in Myth, Religion, and Culture*, edited by Vanessa R. Sasson and Jane Marie Law, 137–56. Oxford: Oxford University Press.

Wall, Robert. 2012. "Reading Scripture, the Literal Sense, and the Analogy of Faith." In *Wesley, Wesleyans, and Reading Bible as Scripture*, edited by Joel B. Green and David F. Watson, 33–46. Waco: Baylor University Press.

Wesley, John. "The New Birth" (Sermon 54). http://wesley.nnu.edu/john-wesley/the-sermons-of-john-wesley-1872-edition/sermon-45-the-new-birth/.

CHAPTER 8

On Dogs and Difficult Texts

Jennifer S. Wyant

Any careful reader of the Bible has Scripture texts they find deeply frustrating, because they do not lend themselves to easy or comfortable interpretations. Oftentimes, there is an impulse to skip over them entirely and move to simpler texts. Yet as a Bible scholar and pastor shaped by the Wesleyan tradition, I have found myself asking how John Wesley might offer a way forward for interpreting difficult texts. In particular, I have long wrestled and struggled with the story in Matthew 15:21-28 of Jesus's encounter with a Canaanite woman—identified as Syro-Phoenician in Mark—who seeks the healing of her daughter. Jesus appears unnecessarily cruel to the woman, though he is kind to so many others who come to him with similar requests.

In this story, Jesus resembles those who judge by appearance, race, ethnicity, and gender, and not the Jesus who came seeking to be in relationship with those people whom society discarded. It is a hard and challenging story for me to read as a white woman living in twenty-first-century America. In this chapter, I apply John Wesley's methods for reading Scripture to Matthew 15:21-28 in order to discover new ways of interpreting it. The goal is not to "fix" my problems with the story, but rather to wrestle something out of it, a deeper truth about God and God's people. To accomplish this, I will first describe Wesley's method for reading challenging texts, as discussed in his Preface to *The Sermons on Several Occasions*, before turning to apply that method step by step to the passage at hand.

Wesley's Method

In order to use Wesley's method, I had to uncover what his approach actually was. My goal was not simply to find how Wesley read Matthew 15, but rather to find specifically what steps he took to interpret passages that challenged him. In his Preface to *The Sermons on Several Occasions*, he writes the following explanation of how he approached reading and studying the Bible:

> Here then I am, far from the busy ways of men. I sit down alone: only God is here. In His presence I open, I read His book; for this end, to find the way to heaven. Is there a doubt concerning the meaning of what I read? Does anything appear dark or intricate? I lift up my heart to the Father of Lights: 'Lord, is it not Thy word, "If any man lack wisdom, let him ask of God"? Thou "givest liberally, and upbraidest not." Thou hast said, "If any be willing to do Thy will, he shall know." I am willing to do, let me know, Thy will." I then search after and consider parallel passages of Scripture, comparing Spiritual things with Spiritual. I meditate thereon with all the attention and earnestness of which my mind is capable. If any doubt still remains, I consult those who are experienced in the things of God; and then the writings whereby, being dead, they yet speak. And what I thus learn, that I teach (Wesley 1771–1794, "Preface," IV).

Wesley considered himself a man of one book (*homo unius libri);* and yet, even he found certain passages "dark or intricate" at times. In this Preface, he describes his method for interpreting them. He begins with prayer and asking God to reveal to him the meaning of the passage. He then reads relevant parallel passages in order to see if those add any insight. After this, he considers the passage closely, attending to its details with "all the attention and earnestness of which my mind is capable." If that is not sufficient, he turns to those people in his life who "are experienced in the things of God." If this avenue also fails, he then turns to the history of interpretation of that passage, reading what the saints who came before him have written about it. In a nutshell, this appears to do what Albert Outler would later call the Wesleyan Quadrilateral since Wesley is using Scripture, reason, experience, and tradition to interpret these passages with which he struggled.

Thus, in this chapter, I apply this four-fold approach to Matthew 15:21-28, adapting it slightly to fit the style of my twenty-first-century biblical training.

First, I pay attention to the text by doing a literary analysis by comparing Matthew's account of the Syro-Phoenician woman with the account in Mark 7, because I believe that Wesley advocates for a *canonical reading* of texts, which is certainly useful in many contexts. Yet for my purposes, *redaction criticism* will be more illuminative, since Matthew appears here to work from his Markan source. Then I will turn to those experienced in the things of God by drawing on the wisdom of womanist and feminist preachers and teachers of Scripture, whose perspectives have often been overlooked in modern commentary traditions. With this approach, I hope, as Wesley suggests, to receive insight into this difficult passage and to be able to teach it faithfully within my own context.

Before beginning this endeavor, however, I must not skip too quickly over Wesley's first step for untangling intricate passages: to pray that God would grant the wisdom needed to understand the text. Very rarely in modern academic biblical interpretation does one find instruction to pray before beginning one's work. But if we truly strive to be Wesleyan biblical interpreters, there is no other way to begin than with prayer.

The necessity of prayer in the Christian life is repeated throughout Wesley's writings. As a means of grace, it is one way in which God reveals Godself to us. Moreover, in his final advice in "A Plain Account of Christian Perfection," Wesley states that: "On every occasion of uneasiness, we should retire to prayer, that we may give place to the grace and light of God and then form our resolutions, without being in any pain about what success they may have" (Wesley 1872). So following Wesley's advice, I too pray that God would grant me the wisdom I need to read this text faithfully.

Paying Attention to the Text

It is easy to lean on what I assume a text says; it is more difficult to pay attention to what is actually there. So, the first step in unraveling a difficult passage is to read what is indeed in the story. Upon examination, we see that this story immediately follows Jesus's encounter with the Pharisees, in which they question him about his disciples' breaking the tradition of washing their hands before eating. The disagreement centers on an argument over what defiles a person, with Jesus explaining later to his disciples that "what comes out of the mouth proceeds from the heart, and this is what defiles" (Matt.

15:18). Jesus then withdraws from that place and heads to Tyre and Sidon, Gentile territory. It is here that our story begins:

Then Jesus left that place and went away to the region of Tyre and Sidon.

> Just then a Canaanite woman from that territory came out and began shouting, "Have mercy on me, Lord, Son of David; my daughter is badly tormented by a demon." But he did not answer a word to her. And his disciples came and asked him, saying, "Send her away, for she keeps shouting after us." He answered, "I was sent only to the lost sheep of the house of Israel." But she came and knelt before him, saying, "Lord, help me." He answered, "It is not fair to take the children's food and throw it to the dogs." She said, "Yes, Lord, yet even the dogs eat the crumbs that fall from their masters' table." Then Jesus answered her, "Woman, great is your faith! Let it be done for you as you wish." And her daughter was healed at that same hour.[1]

After its brief introduction in v. 21, one can loosely divide this passage into four short sections based on Jesus's responses (or lack thereof) to the woman and his disciples:

- The woman's initial plea and Jesus's silence (vv. 22-23a)
- The disciples' request to send her away and Jesus's response (vv. 23b-24)
- The woman's second plea and Jesus's response (vv. 25-26)
- The woman's rebuttal and Jesus's final response/healing (vv. 27-28)

The story repeatedly gives Jesus space to answer in line with the narrative's anticipated outcome that he will heal her daughter, given that Jesus has not yet refused a direct request for healing in Matthew's narrative.

Initially, Jesus simply refuses to respond at all, and he only gives his speech after being goaded not by the woman's constant cries but by the disciples' prompting. When the woman directly asks for help a second time, Jesus again refuses her request, and it is only after she uses the internal logic of his own argument that he finally grants her request. Then at the end we are given a clue into Jesus's thought process and emotional state; Matthew tells us that Jesus is amazed by her faith.

---

1. Matthew 15:21-28 (Author's Translation).

Matthew's source material for this story is Mark 7:24-30 and, like Mark, he inserts this story immediately following Jesus's confrontation with the Pharisees and scribes. Like Mark, he also locates this story outside of the bounds of Israel and includes the dialogue about children and dogs. Both accounts also feature Jesus healing the daughter from afar. Beyond that, however, Matthew rewrites this story in some substantial ways, which bring a new focus to the narrative. It is worth placing the two stories next to each other, so that we can then begin to work systematically through those changes that Matthew appears to make in his account.

Mark 7:24-30 (NRSVUE)	Matthew 15:21-28 (Author's Translation)
From there he set out and went away to the region of Tyre.	Then Jesus left that place and went away to the region of Tyre and Sidon.
He entered a house and did not want anyone to know he was there. Yet he could not escape notice, but a woman whose little daughter had an unclean spirit immediately heard about him, and she came and bowed down at his feet. Now the woman was a gentile, of Syrophoenician origin. She begged him to cast the demon out of her daughter.	Just then a Canaanite woman from that territory came out and began shouting, "Have mercy on me, Lord, Son of David; my daughter is badly tormented by a demon."
	But he did not answer a word to her. And his disciples came and asked him, saying, "Send her away, for she keeps shouting after us." He answered, "I was sent only to the lost sheep of the house of Israel." But she came and knelt before him, saying, "Lord, help me."
He said to her, "Let the children be fed first, for it is not fair to take the children's food and throw it to the dogs." But she answered him, "Sir, even the dogs under the table eat the children's crumbs."	He answered, "It is not fair to take the children's food and throw it to the dogs.
	She said, "Yes, Lord, yet even the dogs eat the crumbs that fall from their masters' table."
Then he said to her, "For saying that, you may go—the demon has left your daughter."	
So she went home, found the child lying on the bed, and the demon was gone.	Then Jesus answered her, "Woman, great is your faith! Let it be done for you as you wish." And her daughter was healed at that same hour.

The first differences are to the setting. Matthew keeps the location in Tyre (and adds Sidon for some biblical flair),[2] but he eliminates the specific setting of a house and the detail that Jesus was hoping to escape notice while he was there. Thus, the woman, when she comes, does not immediately kneel at his feet. Instead, in Matthew's account, she appears to follow behind the disciples, shouting.

Another difference is in the description of the woman herself. In Mark, she is described as a "gentile of Syrophoenician origin" (Mark 7:26). Matthew describes her as a Canaanite woman (Matt. 15:22). Canaanite was the self-designation of people from Syro-Phoenicia during this time, but also by using Canaanite in place of Gentile, Matthew invokes imagery of the outsider in a way that echoes the stories of Israel and their long-time opponents, such as the Canaanites.[3] This shift sets the stage for the reader to know that this woman is an outsider. She is from the people whom God fought against in order to give the Israelites a home and a nation (Deut. 32:49, Josh. 5:12, 14:1). By calling her a Canaanite, Matthew introduces her as part of a historic lineage of those traditionally at odds with Israel, not simply a Gentile. That said, this designation is quickly challenged by her speech. Unlike in Mark, where her request to Jesus is through indirect speech ("she begged him"), Matthew gives us direct speech: "Have mercy on me, Lord, Son of David; my daughter is badly tormented by a demon." As Ulrich Luz points in his commentary, the phrase, "have mercy on me, Lord" echoes the prayer language of the Psalms (Luz 2005, 339):

Be gracious to me, O Lord, for I am languishing;
   O Lord, heal me, for my bones are shaking with terror.
My soul also is struck with terror (Psalm 6:2-3)

Hear, O Lord, when I cry aloud;
   be gracious to me and answer me! (Psalm 27:7)

As for me, I said, "O Lord, be gracious to me;
   heal me, for I have sinned against you." (Psalm 41:4)

---

2. Tyre and Sidon are both discussed as the land of the Canaanites in Joshua and appear linked throughout the Old and New Testaments. They are frequently framed as part of the "wicked" nations throughout the prophetic literature. See Jer. 47:4; Joel 3:4; Zech. 9:2.

3. See Numbers 14:41-45; Deuteronomy 20:16-17; Judges 1:1.

The use of this scriptural speech on the lips of an outsider woman creates tension for the reader. The Canaanite woman uses language similar to the prayers of the psalmists to address Jesus. This makes it particularly disorienting in Matthew's account when Jesus does not respond to her. In Mark's telling, Jesus responds immediately with his statement about feeding the children first. Matthew, however, draws out the encounter by having Jesus ignore the woman and her cries entirely. In this way, Matthew appears to imitate the scene between Jesus and blind Bartemaeus in Mark 10:46-52 (which Matthew does not include in his Gospel). In Mark 10, Bartemaeus follows after Jesus crying out, begging the Son of David to have mercy on him. Matthew incorporates that image here by replacing Bartemaeus with the Canaanite woman.

However, instead of as with the crowd trying to stop Bartemaeus from shouting, in this story, the disciples go to Jesus to get him to tell the woman to go away. The disciples are not present in Mark's account, which is a two-way dialogue between the woman and Jesus. The introduction of the disciples creates a tension point in the story. Unlike Matthew's readers, who are prepared to be sympathetic to the woman, the disciples appear wholly unmoved by her cries for help. In fact, by asking Jesus to send her away, because "she keeps shouting after us," they appear annoyed by her. This is not a sympathetic depiction of the disciples, who, by all accounts, are the insiders.

This leads to Jesus's first statement in v. 24: "I was sent only to the lost sheep of the house of Israel." This is also a Matthean addition to the story, and it can be read both as an answer to the woman, but also as an answer to the disciples who are prompting him to send her away. Jesus's answer echoes the prophets, particularly Isaiah 53:6, which describes how the people of Israel, "like sheep have gone astray," and Micah 2:12, in which God declares that God will bring the remnant of Israel, back "like sheep in a fold, a flock to a pasture." But this is not the first time Matthew has evoked this lost sheep imagery in his Gospel. In Matthew 10, Jesus uses this image while giving instructions for sending the disciples out into the surrounding countryside. While the entire chapter contains Jesus's instructions, this statement here particularly brings to mind Matthew 10:5-8:

> These twelve Jesus sent out with the following instructions: "Do not take
> a road leading to the gentiles, and do not enter a Samaritan town, but go

rather to the lost sheep of the house of Israel. As you go, proclaim the good news, 'The kingdom of heaven has come near.' Cure the sick; raise the dead; cleanse those with a skin disease; cast out demons. You received without payment; give without payment.

Here, Jesus explicitly tells the disciples not to go among the Gentiles, nevertheless in Matthew 15, Jesus has done exactly that. He has gone out of Israel into the land of Gentiles and finds himself telling a Gentile woman that he was sent to the lost sheep of Israel. Once again, this story appears to push against its readers' expectations, shifting who is inside and who is outside. This woman is an outsider, a Gentile, and Jesus was not sent to her. And yet, here Jesus is, in Gentile territory, speaking to her. Meanwhile the disciples (lost sheep if there ever were any) act cruelly, resembling the religious leaders that Jesus rebuked earlier in the chapter. And this woman, who should not know Jesus, follows him and uses biblical language and imagery in her request. Consequently, the story seems to foreshadow the conclusion of Matthew's Gospel, when Jesus commands the disciples to go make disciples of all nations and reminds them that he will be with them even until the ends of the earth (28:19-20). As opposed to Matthew 10, at the end of Gospel, Jesus explicitly commands the disciples to go out into all the nations. The upshot is that by the end of the story, Jesus has no longer been sent only to the lost sheep of Israel, a fact that Matthew's community would undoubtedly already know.

Thus, it is unexpected that the woman is not turned away by Jesus's statement to her and the disciples. At this point she comes up and kneels before Jesus (a detail that Mark includes) and puts forth her second request: "Lord, help me" (v. 25). This phrasing connects her request to the Psalms.[4] Like the psalmists, with their repeated and adamant requests to God, the woman signals that she will not be easily dismissed by what seems to be rejection. Her tenacity prompts Jesus to respond with his infamous statement that it is not fair to take food from the children and give it to the dogs. By adding the previous statement about the lost sheep of Israel, this phrase appears to extend the metaphor—the children being Israel and the dogs being Gentiles. Interestingly the specific Greek word for dog (χυνάριον) only appears in this story

---

4. See Psalm 43:27; 69:6; 78:9; 108:26 (LXX).

in Matthew and Mark. More literally, the word means little dog (sometimes puppy), but it is often used for house dogs or pets as opposed to wild stray dogs who licked Lazarus's wounds, as we read about in Luke 16:21.[5]

The woman is still not deterred, and she cleverly uses and expands Jesus's metaphor. She grants that his premise is correct: the children (Israel) get food first, and she is not a child. She recognizes that she is the dog and does not push back against this idea or argue that it is unfair. Instead, she uses a common trope of feeding dogs from the leftovers from the table. She does not request that anything be taken from the children, the lost sheep, but instead claims "crumbs." With this statement, she wins the exchange and, as such, wins over Jesus who grants her request. He is amazed at her great faith, and her daughter is healed at that very hour.

Jesus's exclamation "Great is your faith!" is an addition to Mark's narrative, and that particular concept is found frequently in Matthew. Most notably in Matthew 8:10, Jesus responds to the centurion (another outsider) who asks for the healing of his servant with the same sense of amazement: "In no one in Israel have I found such faith." Similarly, in chapter 9, Jesus says to both the woman with the issue of blood and the two blind men that their faith contributed to their healing. By listing the woman's faith as the reason for her daughter's healing, Matthew places this story within his larger narrative of the role of faith and how Jesus responds to it.

Thus, we can see that Matthew takes a relatively short Markan account and adds his own thematic elements. He reworks the story so that now it reflects this foreshadowing of how the Gentiles will have access to the *kyrios*, the Lord—the Son of David—and how the woman's faith ultimately qualified her more than her ethnic identity, an identity that might have suggested she was an enemy of God. In fact, in Matthew's telling, the woman is unquestionably the most positive character in the narrative. Her biblical cries to Jesus, her persistence, her faith, and her cleverness when faced with seeming rejection work together to create a powerful image of a mother who will not let Jesus refuse her request. She appears to understand on a deeper level than the disciples what this in-breaking kingdom of God means. She is not dismayed by Jesus's refusal to speak to her or his analogy about the children

---

5. LSJ, s.v. "κυνάριον."

and the dogs. She will get her crumb from the Son of David. In this way, she continues to mirror the psalmists, who also refuse to back down from their requests for God's salvation.

But back to the larger question at hand: Now that I have given careful attention to the text, has "comparing spiritual things with spiritual" helped to unravel some of the intricacies of this text? On one hand, yes; seeing how Matthew constructs this story intentionally to frame the woman positively, even biblically (and against the disciples themselves) adds a dimension to the story previously unnoticed. It has also helped me see how Matthew as an interpreter of Mark understood this story, particularly concerning this foreshadowing of the in-breaking kingdom and its inclusion of the Gentiles. It also shined a light on her faith and her own participation in her daughter's healing.

On the other hand, I still find myself struggling with two issues. First, why does Jesus respond to her with silence and seemingly rebuff her request? She proves herself faithful by refusing to back down, but Jesus does not do this with others who come to him for help. For instance, when another Gentile, the centurion, comes to him in Matthew 8, Jesus quickly agrees to go with him to heal the servant. Why does he ignore her cries? Furthermore, while the metaphor of children and dogs makes more sense within the larger context of the metaphor between Jews and Gentiles, it still stings even if the woman herself does not seem bothered by his statement. Second, I still struggle with how properly to teach this text in a modern context, a central concern of Wesley's biblical interpretation. "What I learn, I teach," Wesley concludes in his Preface. I realize that, although I might be able to walk someone through the literary details of this passage, I am not sure how I would teach this story amid the racial reckoning our country is undergoing. And so I must turn to Wesley's second step of interpreting difficult texts: consulting people who are experienced in the things of God.

Listening to Those Experienced in the Things of God

I am blessed to have a multitude of people whom I consider experienced in the things of God, people whose work I read and study and know personally. That said, for this project, it is prudent to listen specifically to those who would bring a different perspective than my own to the text. After all, my careful attention to the text only got me so far, and I was looking for someone who could show me something that I could not perceive because of my own social location and training. Consequently, I was led to three women who recently wrote about or preached on the story of the Canaanite woman. The first, Mitzi J. Smith, is a professor of New Testament at Columbia Theological Seminary. She has written an essay, "Race, Gender, and the Politics of 'Sass': Reading Mark 7:24-30 through a Womanist Lens of Intersectionality and Inter(con)textuality" in a book on womanist biblical interpretation. She wrote the essay in light of her experiences as a Black woman and as a biblical scholar. The second woman, Tonetta Landis-Aina, is the pastor of Resurrection City Church in Washington, DC and a queer African American woman from the South. She delivered a keynote address on this story in late July 2020 during a conference for Generous Space ministries. The third woman, June Joplin, is a white Baptist minister who preached a sermon, "Persistent Faith" in early August 2020.

Each of these women is comfortable being critical of the text, offering a hermeneutic of suspicion, and yet these critiques are not done by outsiders in attempts to attack. Rather they are delivered by those who are trying to get to the gospel truth of this story amid its difficult aspects. These teachers are wrestling with the story and with Jesus, much like the Canaanite woman. They also approach through the lenses of intersectionality, both their own, and also the intersectionality they find in this story as the Canaanite woman. Specifically, they understand the Canaanite woman to live at the intersection of race, religion, gender, and social status. As a note, while two of these works focus explicitly on Mark 7, they each also engage with Matthew 15 to make their arguments, as the two tellings of this story are difficult to separate from each other fully.

The first thing I noticed from their accounts is how they share my discomfort with Jesus in this story. Joplin refers to this story as Jesus at his most callous, and Landis-Aina goes even further to argue that this Jesus upsets her, because he seems "eerily close to the Jesus of Western white supremacist culture," espousing racial priority, which is so unlike the Jesus she sees in the rest of the Gospel narratives (Landis-Aina 2020, 6:57). Smith, on the other hand, is the most explicit when she argues that Jesus, like all human beings, is a "carrier of oppression" (Smith 2016, 100). Jesus experiences the woman as an outsider, whom he is not called to help. Smith attributes this to Jesus's own cultural experiences as a Jewish male, and she takes his humanity seriously. He is tired and he seeks to be left alone. Joplin similarly focuses on this aspect of Jesus. He is in Tyre to be left alone, and, while she does not excuse his behavior, she notes that it is likely he was drained physically and emotionally, having recently received news of the death of John the Baptist in Matthew 14 (Joplin 2020, 8:02). Jesus's initial interactions with the woman disappoint, but ultimately present him as a product of his culture, which all humans inevitably are. As Joplin summarizes, it is a wrinkle she does not worry much about smoothing out (Joplin 2020).

That said, none of the three theologians spend much time with Jesus and his action, either to let him off the hook, so to speak, or to condemn his action. Instead, they spend most of their time highlighting the Canaanite woman. For them, she is a triple outsider in the story. As Smith observes, "This Greek Syro-Phoenician woman bears a triple stigma because of her race, gender, and status as the mother of a demon-possessed daughter" (Smith 2016, 101). All three of these aspects of her identity are at play in this story and compound her marginalization. Both Smith and Landis-Aina recognize themselves in this stigmatized character, and they can see, mirrored in her experience, their own experiences of being African American women in the South. Smith draws upon the story of Sandra Bland, an African American woman who was pulled over and then arrested, which led to her death in 2015. Landis-Aina references protests against racial violence, which were happening all over the United States when she delivered her address. Joplin also references those protests specifically pointing to the mothers, particularly the Wall of Moms in Portland, who responded to the death of George Floyd in May 2020 and the recording of him calling out for this mother. These modern events provide a lens for each woman as they approach the Canaanite woman and her story.

For Joplin, the Canaanite woman embodies what it means to show persistence in the face of overwhelming bias and oppression, to continue to ask for what you need in spite of continued rejection. Drawing upon the now famous 2017 quote about Elizabeth Warren, the Canaanite woman embodies the statement, "Nevertheless, she persisted." Joplin notes how the Canaanite woman is rejected essentially four times in the story, and yet she comes back a fifth time. She will not be sent away no matter how much it appears that this Jewish healer is not going to grant her request. This persistence is, to Joplin, the real meaning of faith, and that this sort of faith embraces struggle. As she proclaims near the end of her message:

> "Faith is persistent and loud and unfazed by social customs that require politeness and meekness and propriety. Faith does not behave according to rules set by those with power and privilege. Faith does not follow cultural scripts about who is allowed to have a platform and who can speak to whom. Faith does not care whether bystanders are comfortable or not. Faith embraces struggle, because struggle is the path to freedom" (Joplin 2020).

The Canaanite woman is persistent and fights for what she needs. In this way, she embodies better than the disciples do what it means to have faith.

While Joplin draws on persistence, a wrestling with Jesus that she views to be very biblical, Smith and Landis-Aina draw upon the concept of "sass" to define the woman's actions. Sass, according to Smith, is a form of resistance language: "Sass consists of verbal and nonverbal gestures of defiance and resistance. Sass is when the oppressed name, define, call out, and sometimes refuse to submit to oppressive systems and behaviors" (Smith 2016, 97). Sass is more specifically used only by women of color, particularly Black women, as a means of agency, of talking back and resisting invisibility and their own oppression.

Importantly, sass is a tool of the oppressed and is used to resist oppression. Sass, as it is conceptualized here, is not here merely a type of methodology that is equally available to those in power to use as their own and for their own purposes. For these reasons, I do not attempt to use sass myself. Rather, I draw on the insights of women of color who have offered clear definition of it and its usefulness for interpreting the passage at hand. Sass is often a dangerous act when directed at people in power, as seen when Sandra Bland was sassy to the police officer who arrested her, and yet it is an important and subversive form of language. Moreover, Smith sees in the Canaanite woman's response to Jesus's analogy about children and dogs a form of sass. Her response, on one hand, seems to accept Jesus's claim, but on the other hand, subverts it and uses it to her own advantage. In doing so, she resists oppression and is able to claim her own humanity. And in this case, her sass is what transforms the situation. It is her sass that leads to Jesus healing her daughter. Smith argues that by healing her daughter in response to her statement, Jesus affirms her and affirms her inherent power.

What Smith and Landis-Aina show us is that sass, in general, comes from a place of last resort, a place of being exhausted from being constantly faced with one's own oppression and thus, it comes from a place of deep truth-telling needed to confront the lies of oppression in order to strip that oppression of its power. Although it is risky, sass can be a tool for marginalized women to use in order to create a vision of the world where they and their daughters can lead a better life. As Smith says: "But we use our 'mother tongues,' our sass and talk back, for our children, at least hoping they will have a better life and not have to be constrained and demonized by the unclean spirits of racism, sexism, and classism" (Smith 2016, 108).

The Canaanite woman embodies this hope in her sass, and she succeeds because the person she addresses (Jesus) did not value his own traditions and ego more than he valued her life and the life of her daughter. For Landis-Aina, it matters deeply that this woman's sass, her willingness to talk back, was successful. For her, this represents a truth that when one wrestles with and resists oppression, when one refuses to give up when fighting for one's children, real systemic change can happen, and healing can come with it. She discusses her own feelings of hopelessness in the fight against racial injustice, which is seemingly endless with more people killed unjustly because of their race. This story, however, points us to the fact that resistance is not in vain (Landis-Aina 2020). Both Landis-Aina and Smith acknowledge that often real life is much messier than this Bible story that wraps up neatly, and yet it still remains important that in this instance, a woman of color used her sass and saved her daughter.

By reading alongside these three theologians, I was able to recognize the wisdom in Wesley's approach of reaching out to those experienced in the things of God. In particular, their words broke through a logjam that I had when attempting to interpret this text. Their consistent message is that we do not have to solve the problem of Jesus's behavior in the story. It is not a knot that can be untied and to do so would damage to the story as it is. Jesus acts in his human cultural context and reflects his own stated ministry. Smith, Landis-Aina, and Joplin all insist that we do not need to be comfortable with that, but we also cannot ignore it either. Landis-Aina summarizes this idea best when she says, "But the entire story demonstrates what it is not to look away from what is uncomfortable. This, to me, means the whole story is uncomfortable. The genius of it is that because the most problematic parts of the story, the most problematic words come from the mouth of Jesus. We can't actually dismiss them well" (Landis-Aina 2020). To take this story seriously is to engage with Jesus's words and not attempt to make them easier to handle. It is to wrestle with it like the Canaanite woman wrestled with them.

Furthermore, when one does not try to downplay Jesus's words, one is able to better understand the power of the woman, this triple outsider. This allows readers to frame the woman as the hero of the story, who through her persistence and sass, embodied faith and also recast a new world in her reframing of Jesus's statement about dogs and children. I had noticed in my own exegesis the ways in which Matthew frames her positively, but reading with these women allowed me to view her in this new light. She is a woman who uses her voice in a powerful, paradigm-breaking way. She overcomes a system that stands against her, and, in doing so, she foreshadows the in-breaking kingdom of God, one of healing and reconciliation.

Conclusion: What I Learn . . . I Teach?

John Wesley believed that the Scripture is intended to guide lives in the present, and that is what has made the story of the Canaanite woman so dark and intricate. When I read the story of Jesus seemingly dismissing and insulting a woman of color who is in deep need, like Landis-Aina, I am reminded of the terrible racial trauma at the root of our country, a trauma that continues to play itself out over and over again as we say the names of more and more Black men and women extrajudicially killed. We remember Trayvon

Martin, Tamir Rice, Philando Castile, Atatiana Jefferson, Breonna Taylor, Ahmaud Arbery, George Floyd, and countless others. How do I, as a white Southern woman, begin to preach this story with the claim that it should shape our lives?

I am not sure this is what Wesley had in mind, but his approach ultimately helped me. It gave me new insight both into this passage in particular and into my current approach to addressing oppression and racism more broadly. His approach of reading carefully in conversation with other passages, and in conversation with other Christians who have experience with the things of God, taught me to listen to the Canaanite woman. Previously, I was so focused on the "problem" of Jesus's response (and lack thereof) that I did not fully appreciate the strength of her character and how her persistence, faithfulness, quick thinking, and sass represent a new reality, both in the foreshadowing of the kingdom of God in the inclusion of the Gentiles, and also in the way that she, a woman, an ethnic outsider with a demon-possessed daughter, is the one who sees most clearly what God's reign is actually about. She is the last who will be first. She is not silent, passively allowing herself to be dismissed; but in her resistance, she receives what she needs and creates a better world for her daughter. In this way, she understands Jesus and his mission better than the disciples who seek to send her away. The kingdom of God is like a woman who follows after Jesus, praying and demanding he heal her daughter.

She should be allowed to speak to the current moment in American history. Her sass, unlike the sass of so many of Black women in this country, resulted in liberation and healing. In her, we find a reality where women of color receive what they deserve, and this should be the standard that we as people of faith of this country strive toward. We should listen to her voice and to her faith and not seek to hide the power of her narrative behind our own discomfort with Jesus's behavior. We should center her in our telling of this story, her story.

We should center more than just her, however. We should also center the voices and the experiences of women who are constantly placed at the margins. In our context, this means Black women and other women of color. There is a popular phrase, usually spoken around election seasons, that says, "Listen to Black Women." It might sound strange, but what reading this passage through Wesley's lens of difficult Scripture has taught is exactly that: listen to Black women. In a narrow sense, their words helped me understand this passage, to see things I was unable to recognize from my context. But in a broader sense of addressing racial healing in our churches and in our world, we need to listen to Black women. The intersectionality of their experiences of being Black and being female gives them insight into how to fight back against the racism that permeates our culture. Too often their voices are ignored or are criticized for their sass because they are speaking out against the oppression they and their loved ones experience. Their words are a foreshadowing of the coming kingdom of God. Listen to the Canaanite woman, and listen to Black women.

References

Joplin, June. 2020. "Persistent Faith—A Sermon on Matthew 15:21–28." First Baptist Worcester. August 9, 2020. https://www.youtube.com/watch?v=ufjZ8WW0IzM.

Landis-Aina, Tonetta. 2020. "Virtual Retreat 2020 Keynote—Generous Ministries." Virtual Generous Space Retreat. Generous Space Ministries. July 28, 2020. https://www.youtube.com/watch?v=uAuCyNrOLaQ.

Luz, Ulrich. 2005. *Matthew 8–20: A Commentary on the Gospel of Matthew*. Vol 2. Translated by Wilhelm C. Linss. Hermenia. Minneapolis: Fortress Press.

Smith, Mitzi J. 2016. "Race, Gender, and the Politics of "Sass:" Reading Mark 7:24–30 through a Womanist Lens of Intersectionality and Inter(con)textuality." *Womanist Interpretations of the Bible: Expanding the Discourse*, edited by Gay L. Byron and Vanessa Lovelace, 95–112. Atlanta: SBL Press.

Wesley, John. 1771–1794. "Preface." *Sermons on Several Occasions: In Four Volumes*, vol. 1. Philadelphia: J. Crukshank and John Dickins. http://name.umdl.umich.edu/N21366.0001.001.

———. 1872. "A Plain Account of Christian Perfection." In *The Works of John Wesley*, edited by Thomas Jackson. Vol. 11. London: William Nichols. http://wesley.nnu.edu/john-wesley/a-plain-account-of-christian-perfection/.

For Further Reading

Brown, Austin Channing. 2018. *I'm Still Here: Black Dignity in a World Made for Whiteness*. New York: Convergent Press.